Yoruba

The Ultimate Guide to Ifa Spirituality, Isese, Odu, Orishas, Santeria, and More

Your Free Gift (only available for a limited time)

Thanks for getting this book! If you want to learn more about various spirituality topics, then join Mari Silva's community and get a free guided meditation MP3 for awakening your third eye. This guided meditation mp3 is designed to open and strengthen ones third eye so you can experience a higher state of consciousness. Simply visit the link below the image to get started.

https://spiritualityspot.com/meditation

Contents

Introduction

The Yoruba traditional religion has grown in popularity over the past few decades, especially among African-Americans, as this spiritual Ifa system provides a profound sense of cultural belonging. Yoruba is a fascinating tradition made up of myths, lore, legends, indigenous beliefs, traditional songs, and folk proverbs, which are all shaped by the social and cultural contexts of West Africa.

This book serves as the ultimate guide on Ifa spirituality, Isese, Odu, Orishas, Santeria, and more. In it, you'll find in-depth illustrations of the Yoruba tradition, exploring all its elements and influence, and it covers a wide area of one of the most popular and complex of the West African belief system. Learning everything there is to know about this belief system is not something that you can do overnight, especially since there are many terms and cultural contexts people may find very unfamiliar. Fortunately, this book presents the topic in an interesting, easy-to-understand manner. Despite being easy to follow the guide, the book delves deeply into salient topics, ensuring that all the aspects of this spiritual system are covered. This makes it ideal for beginners who have no background in the Yoruba and more experienced individuals who wish to refine and enrich their knowledge.

In this book, you'll find hands-on instructions and methods when it comes to creating an ancestral altar, honoring the ancestors, and making offerings to them, as well as making Yoruba spells, rituals, and baths.

The book provides a thorough introduction to the Yoruba and a brief historical and cultural background. You'll understand how religion didn't wither with the passage of time and remained strong in the face of historical difficulties. You'll also better understand the main Yoruba beliefs and worldview. Then, the book will illustrate insightful details on the Supreme Yoruba God, Olorun, and the creation myth. You'll learn about the creation story and understand how the Yoruba Supreme God manifests himself in three ways.

As you read, you'll be learning about the Irunmole and Orishas and how they can help you, and understand the importance of offerings and how each Orisha has a preferred offering. The book will lead you through the sacred feminine and masculine concepts in Yoruba and present the appropriate deities, along with their origin stories, colors, personalities, and how they were typically worshiped. The following chapter then uncovers the Ifa divination practice and explains who can be an Ifa priest. The book will also walk you through a description of the Yoruba worship calendar and its holy days and how the Yoruba religion managed to influence other African diaspora religions. Finally, you'll find an Orisha offering cheat sheet that you can refer to whenever you need to be reminded of the Orishas and their preferred offerings.

Chapter 1: Introduction to Yoruba

African traditional society, which includes the Yoruba belief system, covers indigenous spiritual concepts and religions of the African population which are not Christian or Islamic. It encompasses a wide array of ritualistic practices, symbols, artistic expressions, customary practices, cosmology, culture, society, etc. If you're a spiritual person, then the chances are that you think of religion as a lifestyle. This is why it only makes sense that African traditional religion and all its elements would have influenced the worldview of the African population.

As opposed to what many people may think, traditional African belief systems are dynamic. They are dynamic and are highly reactive to everything that causes a shift in concepts and ideologies, like aging, technological advances, and the passage of time. These traditional religions are also mostly concerned with life experiences – instead of being doctrine and faith-oriented, they incorporate a multitude of ceremonies, rituals, and other hands-on practices; this makes them incredibly relatable and tangible to those who practice them.

The Triple Heritage

If you read about African religions, you may have noticed that academics usually bring up *triple heritage.* This is because African societies are typically a blend of Christianity, Islam, and indigenous belief systems, which are the *triple legacy.* You may even be surprised to know that even though the people who practice traditional African religion are considered a minority, Christians and Muslims who live in the region are involved in the practices of traditional religions in one way or another. The traditional belief system still influences various aspects of African societies, including its political, social, and economic facets. However, a large portion of the population has converted to Christianity and Islam.

Unlike Christianity and Islam, which are concerned with garnering conversions, traditional African tradition is driven by co-existence. One of its pillars is to encourage peace and harmonious interactions. They encourage the maintenance of good relationships with followers of other beliefs and practitioners of different spiritual activities. While Islam and Christianity still promote the tolerance of all, the followers of traditional African religions don't feel the need to encourage others to adopt their beliefs.

The Influence of Traditional African Beliefs

Few people are aware that these religions have traveled far beyond the borders of their home continent. This diffusion happened during the Trans-Atlantic slave trade and has inspired the emergence of other traditions and belief systems in the Americas, such as the Vodun in Haïti, Santería in Cuba, and Candomblé in Brazil. The relationship and similarities between Yoruba and other religions, including the ones we had just mentioned, will be explored in more depth in the last chapter. African traditional religions' relevance and global reach made these beliefs very attractive to people on diasporic pilgrimages to the continent.

In essence, African religions are particularly interested in reproduction, wealth, and health. This heightened concern is what set off the establishment of institutions and organizations made especially for matters like commerce, healing, and the promotion of the general well-being of the advocates and practitioners of African religions and the members of other religious groups.

Society, Gender, and the Environment

While traditional African religions have set the tone for solid discussions regarding civil religion and society and community interactions, many people still believe that these beliefs conflict with modernity. Unfortunately, this has made minority groups, or the followers of this tradition, subject to inhumane forms of abuse.

Women figure very prominently in these belief systems, which strongly emphasize gender dynamics and relations by highlighting female deities and, to a lesser extent, their divine male counterparts. Goddesses, priestesses, diviners, and other female archetypes are eminent in myths and tales. Modern-day feminist academics even refer to these traditions in their efforts to advocate for the rights of women and their role in African societies. Indigenous African tradition approaches gender in the sense that one is complementary to the other. The forces of the feminine and the masculine must work in tandem.

Another very significant issue is that traditional African tradition discusses our interaction with the environment. These beliefs show a great deal of insight and discernment into how we can live in our environment without causing any harm. This is a topic of great importance in today's world, considering the imminent ecological crisis.

Spirituality and Tradition

Traditional African religions offer robust associations between the realm of ancestors and the world of physical existence. This allows practitioners to keep in constant touch and maintain their relationships with their ancestors. According to indigenous beliefs, our ancestors are highly involved and intricately concerned with our daily life affairs.

Many religions in different parts of the world remain alive through their written texts and recorded scriptures. However, traditional African religion mainly relies on oral story-telling. These tales and oral sources have been elaborately integrated into the social and political structures, various forms of art, and other tangible aspects of culture. Since these traditions are essentially oral, they have left a window for variation and versatility used by various subgroups and multiple other African religions. The Yoruba Ifa tradition and other forms of orature still serve as significant sources of reference when it comes to understanding the religion's practices and its members' worldview.

Reading this chapter will help you understand what Yoruba, a traditional African religion, is. We uncover and try to explain the highly controversial origins and history of this traditional religion – the main Yoruba beliefs and worldviews and how it remained strong in the face of discrimination and disparagement from mainstream religions and societies throughout history.

The Yoruba in a Nutshell

West Africa is home to a group of ethnic peoples known as the Yoruba. As of 2019, there were approximately 44 million Yoruba people, most of whom settled in Nigeria and account for 21% of the nation's population. The Yoruba are among Africa's largest ethnic groups. They have their own language, Yoruba, and occupy other regions and countries besides Nigeria. This includes, but isn't limited to, Ghana, Dominican Republic, Cuba, Jamaica, Saint Lucia, Ivory Coast, Liberia, Venezuela, Brazil, Granada, Sierra Leone, Trinidad and Tobago, and Puerto Rico.

The traditions, spiritual ideologies, and customary practices have all evolved into one solid religious belief system. According to the Yoruba religions, all humans must experience *Ayanmo,* which can be translated into *fate* or *destiny.* This is why this traditional religion suggests that humans will inevitably unite with the divine, the creator and source of all existing energy, in spirit. This state of oneness is called *Olodumare.* Our thoughts, feelings, and actions are translated into interactions with other living entities in the physical realm. Our communications are all efforts to find and attain a destiny in the spiritual world. The followers of the Yoruba traditional religion believe that people who stop experiencing spiritual growth in any of the facets of their lives are bound for *Orun-Apadi,* which is the invisible world of potsherds. The Yoruba religion considers life and death as an endless cycle of existence. Its followers believe that humans constantly reappear in the form of a different physical entity as their spirits gradually develop toward transcendence.

According to the Yoruba belief system, people's destinies are predetermined before they are even born. Their homes, families, partners, career, interests, and even the time and cause of death are all determined beforehand. Followers of the Yoruba tradition believe that a person's plans, destiny, and promises are all forgotten at birth. However, it is also believed that we spend a lot of time and effort trying to remember these things and strive for the future that was destined for us. The Yoruba believers consider god to be the most powerful being and a supreme deity who is not bound by gender. God, or Olodumare, is thought to be living in the skies. Intercessors or Orishas would complete all communications between the Yoruba believers and God.

History and Origins

Ìṣẹ̀ṣẹ is the Yoruba traditional religion name in the Yoruba language. The word Ìṣẹ̀ṣẹ refers to the rituals, customs, and traditions that are widely practiced in the Yoruba cultural scene. This world is a contraction of two words: *Ìṣẹ̀* and *iṣe.* The former can be translated into origin or source, and the latter means tradition or practice. When combined, the words mean *the source of our tradition.* This word was coined to signify the Yoruba belief system because the numerous traditions, practices, observations, concepts, and beliefs are all derived from the spiritual worship of the orisa or orisha. An orisha is a being that withholds the ability to reflect some of Olodumare's manifestations.

Yoruba Traditional Religion

Around 12 to 15 million Yoruba people live in southwest Nigeria, Togo, and the Republic of Benin, which was previously known as Dahomey. These individuals are considered to be the successors of one of the earliest and most prominent West African cultural traditions and belief systems. Linguistic experts and archeological evidence suggest these people have occupied their present-day geographic location since the 15th century BCE, at the very least. Like every other language, regional dialects for the Yoruba language have developed, signifying the urbanization and the distinction between Yoruba subgroups. These differences led to the emergence of a social system in the first millennium BCE. This structure was unique to the Sub-Saharan African population. The traditional home of the Yoruba was thriving by the 9th century BCE. Terracotta and bronze sculptures, which are now among the eloquent riches of Africa, were avidly created by artists over the next five centuries.

Yoruba mythology, oral tradition, and story-telling signify Odudwa, also called Odua, as the founder and first king of the Yoruba people. Some mythologies claim that the traditional home of Yoruba is the cradle of creation and that Odudwa is the god of all creation. However, oral tradition and tales insist that the lore surrounding Odudwa's possession of the throne hints at the conquest led by the people of the east, before the 19th century, of the Yoruba home. Odudwa's followers came up with an urban tradition and increased the archetype or prominence of the king, even though there was a very robust sociopolitical structure of a town under the administration of a king or chief among the subgroups of Yoruba. Later on, those who wished to assert their political validity had to present evidence of their decent or relation to Odudwa, even if they were immigrants. Those individuals were named the *sons of Odudwa*. They wore *adenla* or beaded crowns.

It was said that these crowns were presented to them by Odudwa himself to serve as a representation of their sanctified power.

A Controversial Origin

For years there has been controversy surrounding the ethnogenesis of the Yoruba as both a culture and religion. Numerous historians have studied models to try to determine the origin of the Yoruba population. Much evidence leads back to ancient Egypt. However, it is worth noting that many schools of thought disagree when it comes to the historical analysis of the Yoruba and its traditions. While some historians strongly believe Egypt was the motherland of the Yoruba, others insist that the existence of Arabs and white-skinned Egyptians contradicts the belief that the Yoruba was birthed in Egypt.

It is believed that a source known as the *Ifa Corpus* is a chronicle of all mysteries associated with the presence of the Yoruba people. According to the source, the Yoruba people believe that the supreme God, or the Olodumare, is the creator of the universe and all other deities. Then, Oldumare and the other gods, including Orishanla, the arch-god who was greatly involved in the process, created humans. This is why it's believed that all human civilizations originated in the home of the Yoruba, which is traditionally known as *Ile Ife*. However, various Yoruba ethnogenesis religion-cultural records don't encompass the elements of modern historical methodology. This means that it lacks accurate dating, the pursuit of historical validity and truth, reliable sources, external proof, and structure. This is why it's likely that the information presented by the *Ifa Corpus* is no more than mere lore and mythology.

Even though the different schools of thought affect historical traditions, a very popular trend among modern historians is the heightened interest in the relationship between the Yoruba and ancient Egypt. As we mentioned, it has become a very popular claim that the Yoruba peoples migrated from Egypt. They claim there is evidence of a religious and cultural link between the ancient

Egyptians and the Yoruba. However, aside from the argument regarding the white-skinned Egyptians and the Arabs, many scholars insist there's no solid archeological evidence of the migration of the Egyptians to the land of the Yoruba. If either population had interacted with the other, then, according to historians, it would've likely occurred during the predynastic and dynastic eras, which explains the potential influences.

Additionally, numerous factors may have contributed to the belief that there was direct contact between ancient Egyptians and the Yoruba. This includes colonialism, Islam, Christianity, the Yoruba Creation myth, and the belief that Egypt is the motherland of all human civilization which we will discuss in more depth in the following chapters.

Maintaining Strength

As we mentioned at the beginning of the chapter, practitioners of traditional African religion have been subject to harsh forms of abuse. This is because of the alarmingly dangerous extremism and conflicts associated with Abrahamic monotheistic religions, like Judaism, Christianity, and Islam. These dangers are present within the borders of the African continent and are a looming threat to the practitioners of this religion all around the globe. This terrifying and unjust trend has affected Indigenous southwestern Nigerian Yoruba peoples. Christianity and Islam have unjustly intruded into the lives of the Yoruba peoples, causing turbulence and triggering spiritual imbalance among the traditional religion practitioners. The followers of Abrahamic religions have often conducted waves of forced conversions and actively spoken hatefully toward the believers of other faiths. They treated them as inferior and exposed them to other forms of abuse and prejudice, introducing malevolent characteristics into the society of the Yoruba.

The unwelcome arrival of the spiritual differences into the Yoruba society stimulated religious conflict, but it also led to the onset of superfluous homicide. This was a highly unfamiliar and confusing series of events to the Yoruba, considering their beliefs are fundamentally built on cordial concepts and characteristics like acceptance, harmony, tolerance, and co-existence. The practitioners of that faith are never focused on converting others to their religion or making sure that those around them share the same ideologies and concepts. The extreme efforts to convert members of the Yoruba religious groups rippled disruption, confusion, and feelings of anger and hurt among members of the society. However, the followers of this belief system seem to have managed to stay resilient regardless of the unpleasant disruption.

Another challenge that has acted as a threat to the Yoruba belief system is modernization and rapid technological advancements. All traditions and customs are at a constant threat of disappearance or alteration with the fast-paced nature of today's world. Traditions are typically replaced, forgotten, or entirely lost over time. Fortunately, the West African Yoruba peoples have maintained and kept a strong grip on their traditions. The Yoruba is among the few religious practices and traditions that stay very similar to how it was practiced centuries ago. The Yoruba people have done an excellent job at maintaining their truth.

Lukumi, one of the Yoruba dialects, is the liturgical language of numerous divisions of the subgroups that emerged of the Vodun, Santeria, and Candomble traditions. Nigeria was home to all of these religions. However, they were soon forcefully amalgamated with Catholicism at the start of the slave trade. Slaves were forced to adopt Christianity by their owners and the missionaries. However, their shipment destination was what determined their religious journey and spiritual beliefs. For instance, the slaves that ended up in South America were determined to keep practicing their Yoruba traditions. These traditions were inevitably blended with

Catholicism to form Candomble. Spanish-owned slaves, on the other hand, who ended up in Spain founded Santeria. Lastly, the slaves who found themselves in France created Vodun. The point behind incorporating their current beliefs into their forced practices was to endure survival and maintenance of African beliefs and traditions. It was also a means of protection, as the Yoruba would be subject to harsh and severe abuse or punishment if they were found practicing their traditional religion. In response, they disguised their deities as Catholic saints and continued to worship them. They found saints whose characteristics most resembled their gods and assigned them to the corresponding Yoruba deity. This way, it would look like they were honoring catholic archetypes and celebrating Christian feasts when in reality, they were being loyal to their deities or Orisha. For instance, the Christian equivalent of Shango, the Yoruba king, is St. Barbara. This meant that conducting a drum party for St. Barbara was, in reality, one for Shango.

The determination to keep the Yoruba traditional religious beliefs alive – despite the endless challenges – ensured that we have the information available. Otherwise, the chances are that little would've been known about this belief system today. This is especially true for a religion primarily relying on oral story-telling and tradition.

The Yoruba religious tradition is among the most prominent indigenous African belief systems. This religion is highly versatile and adaptable. It also provides a great deal of insight and wisdom into topics of great importance, even to this day. This is perhaps why it is very relatable and appealing. Despite its complex and controversial history and the multitude of challenges it has faced, this religion has managed to thrive.

Chapter 2: Olorun and the Creation Myth

As you have read in the previous chapter, Yoruba beliefs represent a unique worldview based on spirituality and ancient traditions. This chapter will discuss one of these remarkable views – the relation between the Supreme Yoruba God, Olorun, and the Yoruba creation myth. This religion has its own creation story that's very different from those of other religions past and present. This tale transcended many generations through oral tradition, and the story of creation changed very little and remained faithful to traditions honoring Olorun and the Orishas. It also provides great insight into how the Yoruba see their Supreme God and their relationship with other supernatural beings and mortals.

The Yoruba Creation Myth

Eons ago, when mortals did not yet exist, Olorun and the Orishas lived in the sky - the only livable place at the time. Below them, there was only water, ruled by the goddess Olokun - ruler of the sea. Since the Orishas weren't as powerful as the Supreme God and often needed guidance, they all lived in a close community near a baobab tree. Here everyone found everything they needed to have a happy and peaceful existence. Despite having powers to do much more than that, they lived almost as mortals, tending to their daily needs. The Orishas created everything for their sustenance to pass their days, including stunning clothes and jewelry. They even had had the entire sky reaching above their heads had they wished to see more of their world. However, not everyone was satisfied with their blissful life in their community or wanted to see only the misty sky. Obatala was an Orisha who possessed great powers and an even larger desire to use them to explore far beyond their ruler's land and create something different. Soon, he started wondering what he could do with them, and while doing so, he suddenly looked down and noticed the waters below. It was then that Obatala realized where to begin his new adventure - and he immediately went to

Olorun for permission to build something in the water. He had two reasons for this. Firstly, he needed to create a solid ground on which Obatala himself could stand when he ascended. Secondly, he wanted to make a land for new creatures – someone whom the Orishas could help, so they could finally use their great powers. Seeing that Obatala wanted to do something good and constructive for all of them, Olorun permitted him to descend onto the land of water.

Obatala then consulted another Orisha, Orunmila, about preparing for the journey. Orunmila is said to have divination powers, so he could see everything Obatala may need to make his future quest successful. He conducted a divination ritual by sprinkling powder made of baobab tree roots on a sacred tray. After tossing 16 palm kernels on the tray, Orunmila carefully observed the pattern they left while traveling on the tray. He repeated the process eight times, each time memorizing the kernel markings. His instruction to Obatala was to collect some baobab seeds, maize, sand, and palm nuts to sow and a black cat for company. In addition, Orunimla said to Obatala that the only way to reach the waters was to climb down on a golden chain. He also instructed Obatala to collect personal items from the other Orishas and place them in a sacred egg. At first, Obatala was concerned about finding a gold chain long enough to reach all the way to the world beneath his. He had an idea to go to all the Orishas and ask for their golden jewelry, which he could melt into a chain. He took all the gold given to him to an Orisha known to have exceptional metalsmithing skills. This smith then created a chain long enough to safely help Obatala reach the waters. The chain also had several powerful hooks, so Obatala could secure himself and the items he was carrying with him.

While the smith was making the chain, Obatala went on to find a seashell in which he could gather sand. He then put the cat, the baobab powder mixed with sand, and the maize into the bag and went to look around to find palm nuts and any other seeds he could take with him into this new land. When he gathered everything, Obatala secured the egg to his body with a piece of cloth, ensuring its protection during his climb.

After this, Obatala took the bag with the rest of the items and was almost ready for his journey. His last task was to secure one end of the chain to post in the skies, so he'll be able to climb it safely.

After seven days and nights, his journey came to a sudden halt when he ran out of chain. However, the chain didn't reach the waters yet, so Obatala didn't know how to get lower to the watery kingdom. As he wondered what he should do next, he heard Orunmila calling to him to take the sand from the bag and begin pouring it below him. As soon as he started to spill the sand onto the water, to his surprise, it solidified instantly, creating a firm ground on which he could walk. Unbeknown to him, Obatala had made the egg so warm with his worrying that the spiritual possessions inside it turned into a bird ready to hatch. When it did, a bird named Sankofa flew from it, carrying the spirits of the Orishas. Landing on the solid ground, the bird immediately started to peck at the sand, and the Orisha spirits began to shape the land into mountains and valleys. This is how all these formations got their unique character – they inherited them from the Orishas spirits themselves.

Obatala finally unhooked himself from the chain and let himself drop to the ground when there was land as far as he could see. He decided to name this new land "Ife," which can be translated as the area separating the waters. Eager to explore this new land, Obatala started to walk while shaking his bag and scattering everything from it to the ground. As he did so, the seeds he had in it landed in the soil, and they soon began to grow. In fact, they were growing so fast that they turned everything green without Obatala even seeing this at first. After walking for a long time, he finally turned around and saw palm trees that were already multiplying in his wake.

Obatala had the cat for company, but he still needed to pass his time somehow, so he started to explore what he could make from the palm trees and the other plants growing on Ife. He made wine from the palm trees, but he was bored drinking it alone. One time, while enjoying the wine and fashioning small clay figures, he got the idea to create creatures he could guide and who could also keep him company. The clay figures were not perfect, and he still didn't know how to shape them, so he consulted Orunmila and Olorun. They have decided that the imperfections didn't matter, but the creatures should be shaped resembling the Orishas and not the Supreme Being. It is believed it was Olofi, who suggested this, saying the world needed more Orishas, but there could only be one God. After all, it's the Orishas who deal with nature and living things. As the number of living things multiplied in Ife, there should have been more guides to watch over them. However, not wanting to grant them the same privileges as the creatures living in the sky, Olorun decided to make these new creatures mortal rather than immortal like the Orishas were.

In addition to their physical differences, Orunmila also suggested that the new creatures have different essences. He said some should be better than others, but none should be perfect inside or out. This way, they could learn from their own errors and the mistakes made by others. Although they were to be supervised by the Orishas, the new species should be able to create and keep the balance in nature and amongst their own communities. In addition to this, this new species should know hunger and desire – none of which were familiar to Orishas. Given the enormity of the tasks he has been given, Olorun encouraged Obatala to plant more plants and sculpt other creatures, such as fish, insects, and other animals, before his ultimate goal – humans. All the other creatures could serve mankind as food, and while he was doing this, he would have more time to learn how to create a more physically, intellectually, and spiritually evolved species. Olorun also warned Obatala that humans would also need to have a lengthy period of development to achieve their full potential. Unlike the other species – which may mature in weeks or months – humans will require years of development to learn values such as kindness, sacrifice, and balance.

After some time, curious about what's happening below, Olorun sent another Orisha to see how Obatala was fairing. The report he received said that while Obatala made figures for his entertainment, he still wished they would come to life. He wanted to see them prosper and guide them along their journey. To remedy this, Olorun directed an enormous fireball he made from the explosive gases of the sky to Ife. Not only did this fire help create more habitable land, but it also baked the forms created by Obata. Finally, Olorun sparked life into all the different shapes across Ife using his own powerful breath. After witnessing Obatala's joy with this new life, Olorun sent the fireball back to the sky, where it became the Sun. Realizing Obatala would need help with his task in the future, Olorun sent a couple more powerful Orishas, including Orunmila, to him.

So, Obatala and the other Orishas were doing this grueling work, and they were progressing nicely – at least until it came the time to sculpt the physical shapes of the humans. As Obatala strolled around contemplating how to shape them into the likeness of the Orishas, he got tired and stopped to rest. As he happened to be beside a clear pond, he decided to drink from it. But before actually tasting the water, he noticed his own face – the reflection of an Orisha. Finally, having an idea of what the new forms of life should look like, he immediately started to create them from the bits of clay he found at the side of the pond. Obatala was quite pleased with the end result and made many more clay bodies. He grew thirsty again a couple of times during his work – but he didn't always drink water. Sometimes, he would reach for the wine to quench his thirst, and soon he was quite intoxicated. As a result, the clay forms started to look more and more different, and some ended up missing limbs and other body parts. However, at the time, he didn't notice this, thinking that all his sculptures were beautiful. Besides, he was told the more different they look, the better. That being said, the next time he repeated the process, he did it without drinking wine, so he could focus more on forming them as wholesomely as he could.

Finally, when all the creatures came to life, Olorun descended on the chain as Olofi to see the images of all the living beings. Seeing the vast number of new species, Olofi decided to give each Orisha several of them to guide. Meanwhile, humans were given the task of watching over their natural environment. They were encouraged to report to the Orishas if anything needed changing, although they weren't taught how to communicate their needs. Orunmila created several paths for each human, while others empowered them with different qualities, shaping their final destiny.

Initially curious about the new life evolving around her water kingdom, Olokun didn't interfere with the work of the Orishas. However, seeing how much the new species usurped her domain, she grew angry and decided to take revenge. Taking advantage of the absence of Obatala while he was in his homeland, Olokun commanded her waters to swallow the solid land created by Obatala. The plants, the animals, and many humans died, and only a few people who thought to flee to the highest grounds and ask for help remained alive. They sought refuge and means to survive from Eshu, the only Orisha close by to help. Eshu also agreed to report what was happening to Olorun, but only after the humans offered a sacrifice to both him and Obatala. When Olorun heard what was happening in Ife, he immediately sent Orunmila down again, instructing him to cast spells to make the water retreat. Seeing the drylands reappear again, the human was very grateful to the Orishas and the Supreme God.

However, Olorun decided to empower them even more, seeing that mankind was developing much slower than expected and still could not survive on its own, let alone guard its natural surroundings. He asked Obatala to make them stronger physically and give them larger organs, including brains. Under the tutelage of the Orishas, this newer human species has become more resilient and aware of its surroundings. In addition, the humans were trained how to communicate with their Orishas. They learned which offerings and prayers to make to which Orisha and how to appease them should they make a mishap and disappoint the Orishas or Olorun. Those who weren't taught this yet were under Obatala's patronage, along with all the deformed creatures.

Olorun, Olofi, Olodumare, and the Orishas

While there was now a way for humans to convey messages to the Orishas, they could not do the same with the Supreme God. As the owner of the skies and everything below it, the Supreme God sat at the top of the Yoruba pantheon hierarchy. This ranking was maintained by the three representations of this Supreme God – Olorun, Olofi, and Olodumare.

Olodumare, the almighty, was the maker of the lands – and possibly the creator of the entire universe. However, this being never manifests or receives messages, not even via the Orishas. Its only purpose was to oversee its masterpiece.

Olorun was the only manifestation people could perceive and was always present in the sky, like the Sun. This representation helped maintain the natural order of things and enabled humans to enjoy the world Olodumare created. Apart from owning Orun, the land of spirits, Olorun also communicated with the Orishas but only if necessary.

On the other hand, Olofi was always at the disposal of the Orishas and allowed them to convey messages to and from people.

The Orishas also used this manifestation of the Supreme God as an aid in learning everything they needed to communicate with the people. Thanks to this manifestation, the Orishas could teach them to be more respectful towards others and themselves. It helped them understand how to maintain themselves healthy mentally and physically.

In addition, there are quite a few differences between Olorun and the rest of the Yoruba pantheon. For starters, unlike the Orishas, who can be both male and female, Olorun transcends both genders and is seen as a gender-neutral being. Olorun, as the Supreme Being, rules above everything and everyone else. The Orishas are only assistants, acting as the intermediaries between the Olorun and other beings. Yet, at the same time, for humans, Orishas are just as fundamental as the Supreme God itself. Olorun's energy flows through other Orishas and can't be reached directly.

Yoruba Proverbs and the Significance of Olorun

Ta ní tó Olórum? Edá tá mòla ò sí.

Who is as great as God? No human being knows tomorrow.

This illustrates that no one is more knowledgeable than Olorun. No one knows what destiny holds for them; only Olorun does. So before acting impulsively, it's always worth considering several possible outcomes of your actions. You'll avoid getting into unnecessary trouble.

Eni tí a ò lè mú, Olórum là ńfi lé lówó.

An adversary over whom one cannot prevail, one leaves for God's judgment.

It means that if an adversary is stronger than you, you should let God rule over them. Even if you meet someone causing you great harm, it's best to leave them in God's hands. Olorun will know how to deal with them and will always impart the punishment they deserve.

Olórum ibá dá kan-in-kan-in tóbi tó esinsin, àtapa ni ì bá ta èèyàn.

Had Olorun made the black ant as large as a fly, it would have stung us to death.

By the grace of God, the wicked lack the power to do much harm as could otherwise be possible. Bad qualities are needed to balance out the good. But if not for Olorun, bad people would have no good in them at all, and this balance would not exist.

Chapter 3: Who Are the Orishas and Irunmọlẹ?

In the previous chapter, you learned that the Orishas represent the Supreme God, who created Orishas to help and supervise humankind and other living beings. In this one, you'll learn just how fundamental a part the Orishas play as mediators between the human and spiritual realms and why they represent our most influential source of communication with Olofi - and by extension - Olodumare. Learning about the vast number of Orishas you can turn to will enrich your practice and empower you spiritually, mentally, and physically.

Orishas and Irunmole

However, when discussing the role of Orishas in the Yoruba pantheon, there is another term you must familiarize yourself with – and that is Irunmole. While Orishas are a well-known concept for those who are only somewhat familiar with the Yoruba religion, this is certainly not the case with Irunmole. And those who have heard about the latter often confuse them with Orishas themselves. In fact, there is a vast difference between the two concepts. However, despite the well-documented hierarchy among the different beings of the Yoruba pantheon, parts of the traditional legends about the Irunmole are still missing.

What we know is that the term Irunmole is made up of three words: irun (heavenly being), mo (knowledge), and ile (ground). Therefore, the Irunmole are celestial beings in possession of great wisdom who visit the earth. The word can also be a force of nature, even more powerful than energy. This suggests that they are beings made of light rather than energy. Why is this important? It implies that while most Orishas were human beings who have achieved oneness with Olodumare, Irunmole is the force that gives the Orishas the power to achieve that level. Only those who stand for their actions will become known as Orishas, and this is exactly how Obatala, Oshun, and the other famous figures came to be as well. Irunmole helped them establish the evolution of their energy and spirit into the state of Olodumare. And just as there are many different Orishas, there are many Irunmole, who often work together when helping humans. For example, to overcome a difficult hurdle in life, you'll need assistance from Ogun, and the Irunmole Ogun, too.

According to some Yoruba sources, the first 200 Orishas created by Olodumare already possessed Irunmole. In fact, it's possible that these Orishas suggested the creation, including those inhabiting the earth. Initially, they were the only intermediaries between Olofi and mankind, but it is easy to understand their use of their powerful energy to help other creatures. They were also able to take on many forms, much more than some of the lesser Orishas. They formed the celestial community in the skies and regularly called on the Supreme Being, consulting it about their daily duties. As legend has it, they visited so often that Olorun decided to give them a special task to have more peace around the baobab tree. So, when they asked about expanding the universe towards the waters below, Olorun was more than happy to send them to Ife to supervise the evolution of the new life.

Nowadays, an Irunmole is said to be the only presence of the Supreme God on earth. Despite this, it's still capable of maintaining several spiritual and physical forms, including humans and even inanimate objects. According to many contemporary Yoruba practitioners, Irunmole may also empower incorporeal entities if their help is needed during a spell or ceremony. Some of them also consider Olofi as the first Irunmole, which explains why he is the only manifestation of God who communicates with other species. However, all of them agree that, unlike Orishas, Irunmole were never human beings but natural spirits. This is why they can become manifestations of divine power, natural or spiritual energy, or any driving force humans need but find incomprehensible. Only by moving away from their abstract description can one truly understand their importance in human lives. Whether you think of them as spirits of energy and light or highly achieving Orishas with special abilities, they can help you develop and transform your energy, raising it to a much higher plane. Overall, 401 Irunmole are wandering the earth looking for humans to help. If you decide to seek assistance from them, don't forget that you may need the help of a lesser Orisha to facilitate communication with them.

Whereas the Irunmole are seen as light entities, the Orisha are nowadays thought of as almost like humans. Each of them is associated with an aspect of nature in which they express their divine qualities. They can accomplish exemplary feats – which are duly recognized – yet humans can communicate with them. Of course, one must know how to honor an Orisha. Otherwise, they won't work with you. You must learn what they like and don't like to avoid getting on their bad side. While they often work as the intermediaries between man and Olofi or the rest of the divine world, the Orishas can sometimes work against humans as well. Much like humans, they have their likes and dislikes, and if something angers them, they can do just as much harm as they do good.

While this changeable mood can seem like an off-putting quality, this human attitude makes them so relatable. We can see they have their own flaws and virtues, just as we do, and new practitioners are always advised to look for an Orisha they can relate to best. Working with an Orisha allows you to form a personal connection with them. You gain a guide and a counselor in a being you can identify with, and the more you get to know them, the stronger your bond will become. It's also a quality that contributes to the continuity of this belief system, not forgetting its influence on the development of so many contemporary African and South American religions. Fortunately, there are many Orishas a Yoruba practitioner can turn to, and this book will discuss the most important and helpful ones in the following chapters.

Each Orisha has its own prayer bead or eleke and numbers in Yoruba culture. And, despite there being so many, they even recognize each other from their number. Some of them are said to have been present as Irunmole when the earth was created from the ancient water kingdom, while others have come into being much later. These were most likely human beings themselves, who transcended into a semi-divine existence. Each Orisha communicates and manifests differently. Some appear as natural landmarks, such as mountains, rivers, or trees, while others emerge as familiar human beings or animals. According to the ancient

Yoruba legends, Orisha didn't know hunger, thirst, and desire at one time as these are all unfamiliar to celestial beings. However, as their numbers grew and they spent more and more time with mankind, they gained the ability to eat, drink, and love – just as humans do. They have also learned to enjoy music, making them easy to appease.

Moreover, each of them has their own favorite foods and other items they like to receive as offerings and gifts. Suppose you make an offering to an Orisha in a way they are accustomed to, and you offer them something they like. In that case, they will recognize the gesture and come to your aid right away. The research will teach you more about their likes and dislikes, and observing the forces of nature they govern is even more helpful. When you conduct your research, remember that Orishas often work together, so you should always observe how the forces of nature interact with each other. For example, the Orisha ruling over rivers will work with the one governing the seas that the rivers flow into. The way the river flows and its rising and falling also reflect Orisha's changeable mood. As you observe their work, you'll get a better understanding of the complex ways of the Orishas. You'll see their celestial force, as well as their human qualities. This will empower you with the knowledge that they are in a way no different from you, making it that much easier to form a deep bond with them. If you manage to establish a mutually respectful relationship with an Orisha, one day, when you need them the most, you may come face to face with them.

Orishas and Ashe

Although their role as messenger between the Supreme God and us cannot be denied, the Orishas can be even more helpful in healing practices. The Orisha's Ashe can subdue misfortune and evil, cleansing your soul and helping it grow until you reach the desired level. For many, this means achieving oneness with Olodumare, but even if your goal is to heal past wounds - Ashe will be of great assistance.

But what is Ashe, and how does it affect you? Ashe is a divine power, the driving force behind everything in the world. Initially, Olodumare gave this energy only to Orisha's living and serving God in the skies. Even when they came up with the idea of creating Ife and humankind, the man wasn't gifted with Ashe as it wasn't deemed necessary for them to have it. Over time, the Supreme God and the Orishas realized that every living being could benefit from this force. For this reason, the Supreme God begins to empower everything with Ashe, including inanimate objects, making it one of the most fundamental concepts in the human belief system. Now, we know it as the immense power behind everything, including our own thoughts, emotions, and actions.

However, Ashe comes to us through only one source - the Orishas. They are the custodians of this flow and can channel it towards us, so it carries us on our journeys. By working with Orishas, you can draw on their Ashe through prayers, offerings, and other ceremonies - ensuring that you stay on the right path. In addition, there are other ways to channel Ashe towards you, particularly for divination or healing. Herbs, colors, candles, and crystals can also initiate its flow towards you, conducting it into you and uniting it with your own energy.

Working with Ashe might be easier than you think, as it is accustomed to receiving voiced words such as prayers, songs, curses, and praises. Sometimes, even an everyday conversation can attract it, encouraging you to make things happen and achieve the change you wish for in your life. For the same reason, you must be very careful how to use it; your entire existence may depend on it! Not only does Ashe have sacred characteristics, but its social ramification often goes beyond anything imaginable. Anyone who learns how to experience and use this essential life force becomes an authority figure. At the same time, through their own initiation, they become subject to its wilful effect that changes their lives forever. You may learn to command this power, but you'll depend on it even more. Except, now you'll know how to employ it in your rituals when invoking particular Orishas or even Olofi should you need their help. Working with an Orisha means recognizing the uniqueness of their Ashe and knowing when they may be useful for you. Recognition of their autonomy is also a sign of respect, which in turn, will earn you their trust and a much more amicable relationship with them.

How Do the Orishas Heal?

When an Orisha comes in contact with your body, it transfers its Ashe to you. However, apart from lending you their Ashe to make you stronger and overcome difficult hurdles in life, Orisha can assist you in many other ways. Each Orisha represents a particular force in the Yoruba pantheon. They all have their own specialties, but they also have specific influences. They can protect and heal nature, and they can do the same for you – you just have to know which one to call upon. According to the powers of the one you choose to work with, an Orisha will protect and defend you, or it may cause disease to go away from the affected part of your body. From physical ailments to emotional scars – we all need healing in many different ways. And while the bond you form with an Orisha will mainly be manifested in your body, this doesn't mean it won't empower your mental state. You exist through your body, so this is the only way the Orishas can connect with you. But once the connection has been made, they will envelop your mind and body, healing you spiritually, if necessary. As mentioned before, you'll most likely need some intermediaries to transfer the energy. Using elements associated with the Orishas will encourage their interaction with your body, ultimately restoring its health and vitality.

What Is an Ebo?

In terms of Yoruba terminology, ebo means sacrifice. However, an ebo can mean a lot of different things as well. It can be offered during different ceremonies and may represent several types of sacrifices. It can be performed as a sacrifice, offering, purification, or an expression of gratitude. Furthermore, the ebo made at each event will depend on the Orishas you are calling on and their likes and dislikes. After a traditional Yoruba ebo, the power of every prayer, spell, or ritual is elevated, and the practitioner's mindset will be focused on manifesting a positive outcome.

There are many types of ebos, and they can be identified by the elements used in them, the offering, and the process used to make the offering. While animal sacrifices were a common occurrence in the past, they aren't required nowadays. The Orisha you call on will be satisfied with a simple offering of fruit and sweets, accompanied by a prayer or perhaps a bath and a display of flowers. Remember, during an ebo, you are cleansing your body from negative energy so that the Orisha's ashe can flow through it more freely. It is considered a medicine that can heal past wounds and solve problems. This is only possible if the sacrifice you make serves your tranquility and health, both physically and mentally. Even if you only do it as a way to please an Orisha in hopes of further collaboration, it will only work if you are keeping a balance in nature as well. After all, the Orishas watch over other beings, not just humans.

Ebo is a common ritual performed prior to the Ifa divination. In this case, it's a combination of rituals that symbolically prepares the person needing the divination. But an ebo is often essential in other types of situations when you want to change your circumstances. Apart from cleansing, an ebo can help identify issues within your spiritual makeup. Having found them, you'll be able to heal them and feel better. Whether you wish to reveal your future or someone else's, need guidance in achieving goals, or seek spiritual enlightenment via the traditional Yoruba ways, you must perform an ebo beforehand. Even if the person for whom the ceremony is performed is in tune with their destiny, performing an ebo will maintain the natural balance of energies.

The ebo sacrifice (or eje) is a specific type of ebo and represents offering the highest power within a living being. While some interpret this as using the blood of an animal, this is far from the truth. In fact, the power and the Orishas ashe flows through the entire animal, and it's the strongest when the animal is alive. This is why many practitioners use living animals during their rituals. For example, you may choose to adopt an animal and nourish its life force, promoting the flow of ashe through it even more. Or you can give it to the person for whom you are performing a ritual so they can take care of it. Another type of animal sacrifice is releasing the creature into nature after the ceremony is concluded. Or the release itself may be fundamental for the ritual's success. This is a common practice in group cleansing rituals before a major festival. Another ebo in which entire communities partake in the celebratory feast. The animals aren't sacrificed in vain but cooked and used as sustenance. It is an act of gratitude towards the Orishas, nature, and the animal that gave its life to feed the people. This is an act that brings harmony and balance into the community and into the life of its individual members.

Chapter 4: Main Female Orishas

We have talked in the previous chapter about Orishas and their role in the Yoruba religion. Up to this day, the Yoruba gods still fascinate people. As the intercessors between the Supreme Deity and humans, the Orishas play a huge role in the Yoruba religion. There are different types of Orishas, and they represent the forces of nature. As mentioned in previous chapters, there are male and female Orishas. In this chapter, we will focus on the main female Orishas.

Ayao

Ayao is the goddess of the air. She lives in the forest or in the sky, and when she travels, she becomes a cyclone or whirlwind. Ayao never touches the ground; for this reason, all her ceremonies take place on a table. She is given to Oya's children, but nowadays, she is given to priests and priestesses. When Oya initiates perform a blessed birth, Ayao tends to the spirits they collect. She uses these spirits to help her sister Oya in battles.

- **Origin Story**

  Ayao is the younger sister of Oya, who is another Orisha. She and her sister are highly revered. Ayao lives in the sky to protect the spirits who go through her clouds to live in the Olofi kingdom. She works with the nature Orisha, Osain, from whom she learned magic and botanical knowledge. She uses nine stones, a crossbow, and a quill.

- **Personality**

  Ayao is a very powerful and fierce warrior. She is known as a very smart Orisha, and she has an abundance of magic knowledge and witchcraft.

- **Colors**

  You'll find the colors associated with Ayao are the colors of leaves and barks – different shades of brown and green.

Oya

Oya is the goddess of the weather. She represents storms, hurricanes, and wind. She is a tall and beautiful woman. She is one of the seven African Powers; she is one of the most powerful and feared Orishas. Women call on this Orisha to help them resolve disputes, which is why she is considered a protector of women. She guards the underworld to help transition the newly dead from our world to the spirit realm. She is also associated with funerals. By rotating her skirt while dancing, Oya can summon tornadoes and lightning. She can alter the cosmos, which is required to bring balance to the universe. Oya can manifest as a beautiful woman or a horned water buffalo. Mothers who suffer from miscarriages and want to get pregnant offer drinks and food to Oya. She cures lung diseases and protects against tornadoes, storms, hurricanes, and lighting. She can also protect the living from being haunted by the dead.

• Origin Story

According to a Yoruba legend, one day, Ogun, the god of war and iron, saw a striking horned water buffalo coming out from the Niger River and transforming into a very beautiful woman. He followed her as she walked like a royal – and couldn't help but fall in love with her. He begged Oya to marry him, but she was hesitant. However, Ogun told her that he knew about her bovine identity and threatened to reveal it if she didn't agree to marry him. They got married, and he loved her passionately. However, during an argument, Ogun accidentally revealed her secret. Oya then left him and married his brother Shango, the god of thunder and lighting. She was his trusted advisor and would fight side by side in battle. However, Oya was barren, so she sacrificed a piece of cloth with the colors of the rainbow. It worked, and she gave birth to 9 children.

- **Personality**

Oya is extremely intellectual and powerful. She is a brave warrior who never backs down from a battle. According to legend, she would grow a beard and wear pants to fight like a man during wars. She is a strong protector, especially to her children, and has helped out every Orisha. This powerful Orisha can summon any natural disaster to destroy men, lands, and cities when angered. She also has psychic abilities that enable her to see things beyond our world.

- **Colors**

The colors associated with Oya are black, reds, oranges, maroon, and shades of purple.

- **Food and Offerings**

Oya prefers fruits like purple grapes, purple plums, back grapes, and starfruit. However, her favorite food is eggplants, so a traditional offering for Oya should be nine eggplants. Simply cut one eggplant into nine pieces if you can't afford nine, and nine is the number associated with her since she has nine children. Other offerings for Oya include flowers, red wine, bean fritters, legumes, and tobacco. You can present the offerings by bringing them to cemetery gates or setting up an altar at your home. The best meal for an Oya ritual is nine bean soup or eggplant with rice.

Yewa

Yewa is Oya's sister, and like her sibling, she is also associated with graveyards. She is the goddess of death and virginity. She works with Oya and lives in the cemetery. Yewa is considered the queen of corpses, as she protects them from the moment they die until they are buried. She then delivers them to Oya. According to legend, Yewa would dance over the graves to reassure the dead and let them know they were protected. She also protects the innocent and punishes anyone who disrespects the cult of the dead. It is also believed that Yewa would transform into an owl to perform her guarding duties unnoticed. Since she is also the goddess of virginity, her devotees must remain celibate.

- **Origin Story**

Yewa wasn't always the goddess of death; she used to be a water Orisha. She is the daughter of Obatala, the sky father and the god of purity, and was known for her exquisite beauty. According to legend, Shango, famous for being a womanizer, seduced Yewa when she was very young and got pregnant. However, she was given a potion that caused her to abort the child. She was devastated by the incident and punished herself by residing in the cemetery. However, there is another version of the myth; it said that she loved Shango but didn't give in to her feelings and remained a virgin. She was ashamed of her feelings and confessed to her father, and he sent her to the realm of the dead, where she remained a celibate.

- **Personality**

Yewa is mysterious, shadowy, and very regal. She has a very serious personality, and she despises humor, promiscuity, and sexual banter. She also hates cursing, vulgarity, foul language, sexual innuendoes, and any sex discussions, which makes sense since she is the goddess of virginity. Yewa is considered one of the most reclusive

Orishas, and she is very diligent, intelligent, wise, knowledgeable, and hardworking.

- **Colors**

The two colors usually associated with Yewa are scarlet and pink.

- **Food and Offerings**

As the goddess of death and the queen of cadavers, Yewa would appreciate scented flowers to cover up the odor of dead bodies. You should opt for a large bouquet of flowers to increase the fragrance.

Oba

Oba is the goddess of rivers, and water is her symbol. She represents energy, flexibility, protection, and restoration. In some places, she is considered the goddess of love, while in others, she is the protector of prostitutes. She punishes anyone who takes advantage of a loving heart, just as she was misled while loving her husband – who could not stay true to one woman.

- **Origin Story**

The story of how Oba became the goddess of the River is a very sad one. She was Shango's first wife, but she was aware of her husband's wandering eyes. She didn't mind sharing him as long as she remained his only queen.

However, Shango fell madly in love with Oshun and Oya, and he treated them like queens. Oba was extremely frustrated and jealous of how her husband loved these women. According to legend, one of the women tricked Oba and told her that she cut off a piece of her ear, cooked it, and served it to Shango, making him desire her. Oba decided to follow in her rival's footsteps and cut off her ear to serve it to her husband. However, when Shango saw the ear on his food, he was disgusted. Some legends say he left her and never returned, while others say that he thought she wanted to poison him and kicked her out of the house. She then kept crying until her tears created the Oba river. It isn't known exactly *which of the women* tricked Oba, but Oshun was famous for her cooking skills.

- **Personality**

Judging by her sad story, you may think Oba is stupid or weak. However, Oba is a very intelligent woman who is also independent and plays a huge role in politics and commerce. She is also powerful, beautiful, and wealthy. She was just outsmarted by a cunning woman who took advantage of her love for her husband.

- **Colors**

The colors associated with Oba are red, white, and pink.

- **Food and Offerings**

Oba Orisha prefers flowers, wine, candles, and pond or lake water. Avoid rainwater and spring water. If you plan to cook a meal for this Orisha, opt for beans with shrimp and onions.

Yemoja

Yemoja, who also goes by the name Yemaya is the goddess of the ocean's surface. She represents motherhood and all issues concerning women. She is one of the Seven African Powers. The name Yemaya means "the mother whose children are fish." This name signifies the many devotees she has, which are as numerous as the fish of the sea. Additionally, she has many children since she is the mother of almost all the Orishas. She lives in the sea and is associated with saltwater.

- **Origin Story**

Yemoja is Oshun's sister. She used to live in the graveyard while Oya lived in the sea. Yemoja tricked Oya into trading places with her. Oya never forgave her, which is why these two Orishas should never be revered together.

- **Personality**

Yemoja has many devotees as a result of her kindness and generosity. Her personality resembles that of the sea; she is giving, beautiful, profound, and filled with treasures. However, just like the sea, you should avoid making her angry. She also likes to keep everything and everyone she loves close by.

- **Colors**

The colors associated with Yemaya are white, pearl, and blue.

- **Food and Offerings**

To appease Yemaya, opt for perfume, seashells, coral, jewelry, flowers (her favorite are white roses), and scented soap. When it comes to food, this sea goddess prefers watermelon, pomegranate, and all other wet seedy fruits and vegetables. She also enjoys proteins like duck, fish, and lamb. Yemaya prefers coconut cake, pork cracklings, banana chips, and plantain for snacks. You can place the offerings in the ocean or build an altar at your home.

Osun

Osun, also spelled Oshun, is the goddess of the river. She is one of the female deities of the Seven African Powers. She represents love, romance, beauty, and wealth. She dominates anything that flows like honey, water, milk, and even money. Osun has healing abilities for the reproductive organs, among other human body parts. She is usually called on to help with fertility issues and to provide employment, protection, wealth, and love. Oshun usually manifests as a gorgeous woman or a mermaid. She always carries a mirror with her to admire her own beauty.

- **Origin Story**

According to Yoruba legends, Oldumare, the supreme god, sent male gods with Oshun to create a world on earth. However, the male gods were dismissive of her and her help. Oshun grew tired of not being appreciated and decided to leave. She resided on the moon, where she could be by herself to admire her beauty. She expected the male deity to ask for her help soon. She wasn't wrong, though; everything on earth started to wither, including animals and plants. Oldumare informed them that Earth needed Oshun's love and beauty to survive. The gods begged her to come back, and she did, and the Earth thrived again. It is believed that she is either Yemaya's sister or daughter; for this reason, they are usually venerated together. This isn't the case for Oshun and Oya, though, since both women were married to Shango.

- **Personality**

Oshun isn't only extremely beautiful, but she is also a powerful warrior. Although she is the sweetest and smallest, Orisha is very tough. She helped Ogun get out of his depression, and she is the only Orisha able to fly to heaven to speak with the Supreme God. Oshun is very generous and incredibly forgiving, which is why she was able to quickly forgive the male deities. She rarely gets angry, but she can be extremely dangerous and hard to appease when she does.

- **Colors**

Oshun is associated with the colors orange, yellow, and gold.

- **Food and Offerings**

For the beautiful Oshun, focus on feminine items like brushes, mirrors, perfumes, or makeup. This deity of love would also appreciate flowers. You can also offer her fans made from yellow sandalwood or peacock feathers. When it comes to food and drinks, Oshun loves chamomile tea, and her favorite meal is spinach with shrimp. You should opt for honey if you want to please her since it is her favorite offering. However, you must taste it first, or else the offering will be rejected. This is because someone once tried to poison Oshun with poisoned honey. She also loves orange and yellow vegetables and fruits.

Olokun

Olokun is the deity of the sea. They provide healing, wealth, and fertility. This Orisha's gender, identity, and function vary according to different myths. According to Nigerian legends, Olokun is the king of the sea. He is very powerful and rich, but he didn't survive the Middle Passage slave trade.

- **Origin Story**

According to another legend, Olokun is female and is either Yemaya's mother, alter ego, or sister. As mentioned, Yemaya is the Orisha of the surface of the sea or ocean, and Olokun is the goddess of the deepest and darkest parts of the sea. She is the Orisha of life and death. It is believed life emerged from the sea, and the realm of death is at the bottom of the sea. Olokun controls the area souls have to cross to either be born or return to death's realm. Olokun can heal pain and any kind of abuse, whether physical or mental. Her abilities extend to healing pain and abuse that occurred before birth or speech.

- **Personality**

Olokun prefers to be alone, and she is usually silent and brooding.

- **Colors**

The colors associated with Olokun are beige and blue.

- **Food and Offerings**

This Orisha prefers offerings related to the sea like saltwater and seashells.

Nana Buruku

Nana Buruku is the supreme goddess, the creator, and the great grandmother of all the Yoruba deities. She is the most respected and admired Orisha, and she represents swamps, mud, clay, and marshes. She is usually called on to help provide medicinal herbs that can heal various ailments. She can also identify and cure diseases that doctors can't understand or treat. Additionally, Nana Buruku is called on by people who suffer from infertility. She also guards the dead and manifests as a very old woman.

- **Origin Story**

According to legend, this supreme goddess gave birth to the sun (Lisa) and the moon (Mawu). Afterward, she retired and entrusted the world to her children. It is believed that Nana Buruku used magic to create humans and the cosmos, and her twin children were the first man and woman.

- **Personality**

Nana Buruku is a very brave warrior and a fierce witch. Her generosity knows no bounds when it comes to the people she loves. However, you should never anger her, or she will infect you with diseases.

- **Colors**

The colors associated with this supreme deity are white, black, pink, and dark blue.

- **Food and Offerings**

To appease Nana Buruku, focus on plant-based offerings like roses, swamp plants, mandrakes, or any other roots.

Abata

Abata is the Orisha of marshes and swamps. She has the power to make someone either wealthy or poor. She usually controls places where saltwater and freshwater merge, like in swamps. She can provide emotional balance, health, and peace.

- **Origin Story**

According to Yoruba legends, Abata is the wife of Erinle, the Orisha of wealth. However, other legends believe she is his counterpart, and they can merge together. Unlike her husband, there isn't much known about her. This is probably because she is a swamp, Orisha, and swamps are usually associated with hidden treasure and secrets.

- **Personality**

Abata is very powerful and hardworking. She is famous for her vast knowledge as well.

- Colors

The colors associated with Abata are the shades of her necklace beads: green, blue, and yellow. Other colors associated with her are gold, coral, and pink.

- **Food and Offerings**

Abata's favorite food includes roasted yam, sweet potatoes, and snapper. She also enjoys panetela, almond oil, sweet guava, and almond balls. She will be very pleased if you offer her white wine since it is her favorite drink. She also likes fruits and flower arrangements, melons, and grapes. Abata prefers her offerings to be brought to her home in the swamps.

Aja

Aja is considered one of the most popular Orishas. She is the goddess of forests and animals. She is also a healer who uses the medicinal plants in her forests to heal the sick. Aja loves sharing her knowledge which is why people like shamans call on her to bestow her knowledge on them. Aja isn't like other Orishas because she will reveal herself to humans with no intention of scaring or harming them but teaching them how to make healing herbs.

- **Origin Story**

Aja lives in the forest, where she makes potions to help the sick. According to legends, she is the wife of the sea god Oloku and Yemaya's mother.

- **Personality**

Aja is a healer and a strong warrior who shouldn't be provoked.

- **Colors**

Since she is the Orisha of the forest, Aja is associated with the color green.

Chapter 5: Main Male Orishas

The Yoruba religion, which originated in West Africa, is home to a plethora of deities and supernatural creatures, including supreme beings and the Orishas, the intermediaries between mankind and the divine. Previously, we learned of the female Orishas; this chapter covers their male counterparts. Male Orishas are best understood through examining the natural forces with which they are associated.

Aganjú

In Yoruba mythology, Aganju is associated with volcanoes, the wilderness, and rivers. Thought to be one of the oldest of the Orishas, Aganju is rumored to be the third deity who came to earth. Aganju is considered a cultivator of growth and civilization, both of which are linked to his symbol, the sun. Like a volcano, Aganju can bring about a drastic change in society and is the foundation upon which societies are built.

- **Origin Story**

Aganju was supposedly a king in the Oyo Empire in Yoruba history. He was the fourth Alaafin of Oyo (which means "owner of the palace" or king in Yoruba) and was greatly loved by his people. Before he ascended the throne, he was a warrior and used to carry a double-edged sword everywhere with him.

- **Personality**

He loved nature and used to explore the wilderness for days. One time, he came back with a leopard and domesticated it. Even while living among humans, Aganju was no ordinary man. He was rumored to have spiritual and unimaginable powers and an ability to domesticate wild animals.

- **Colors**

The colors (or, more accurately, the *bead pattern*) associated with Aganju are two brown, one red, one yellow, one blue, one yellow, one red, and two brown.

- **Food and Offerings**

Aganju likes offerings of alcoholic drinks and beef food items.

Babalù Ayé

Associated with disease and healing, Babalù Ayé is considered the spirit of the earth. Consequently, he controls everything earthly, including health, wealth, and any physical assets. His name roughly translates as "Father, Lord of the earth." In earlier Yoruba beliefs, he was mainly linked to smallpox, and other epidemics, whereas modern Yoruba beliefs associate him with AIDS, influenza, and other infectious diseases. Although most people associate Babalù Ayé with the disease, he is also the patron of healing and is both feared and loved.

- **Origin Story**

From the ancient Yoruba mythology folklore, Babalù Ayé's origin story is commonly retold by many Yoruba followers. Once, Shopona (common name for Babalù Ayé in Yoruba tradition) attended a party at the Orisha's, where he stumbled and fell. When the other Orishas laughed at him, he tried to inflict smallpox on them but was stopped and exiled by his father.

- **Personality**

Although many beliefs in Yoruba depict Babalù Ayé as someone to fear, he is also a merciful and humble Orisha. He is associated with healing as much as with disease. He also helps people with terminal diseases to get peace by guiding their souls to the other side.

- **Colors**

The sacred colors associated with Babalù Ayé are blue, yellow, and purple.

- **Food and Offerings**

The food offerings Babalù Ayé favors are black-eyed peas, beans, popcorn, rum, and tobacco.

Erinlẹ̀

Erinlẹ̀, commonly known as the elephant of the earth in Yoruba, is considered the deity associated with healing, medicine, and comfort. One of the most fiercely celebrated Orishas, Erinlẹ̀, is the underwater king, as well as the spirit of the bush. Erinlẹ̀ has two sides, as a water spirit and healer – and a hunter of the forest and a warrior.

- Origin Story

According to Yoruba tradition, Erinlẹ̀ was a hunter before he became an Orisha. He is said to have protected the town of Fulani from attackers. He used to live in the forest, in a hut he had made for himself. Some myths claim that one day he sank into the earth near Ilobu, where he first conducted Olobu and became a river.

- Personality

Envisioned as one of the wealthy deities, he is dressed in luxurious and beautiful clothes, combined with accessories from the sea and forest. As a deity associated with earth, he is masculine and mighty.

- Colors

Being associated with rivers and the forest, the colors of patron Erinlẹ are turquoise, coral, and green.

Èṣù

Èṣù, pronounced Eshu, is considered the trickster Orisha in Yoruba tradition. He is full of tricks and pranks that can often be cruel and are sometimes harmful. Known to speak all the languages on earth, the messenger deity, Èṣù, conveys messages from the gods to people. He's also said to carry the offerings people send to different Orishas.

- Origin Story

Yoruba mythology tells of how Èṣù became the messenger. Due to his love for pranks and tricks, he played one on the high god, in which he stole his ham, used his slippers to make footprints, and tried to convince the high god that he stole the ham himself. The god got annoyed and told Èṣù to visit the land every day and tell him about the occurrences at night.

- Personality

Èṣù is an embodiment of mischief and loves to cause trouble. He likes to be appeased to fulfill his duties of conveying messages to and fro. This deity often makes use of trickery to teach lessons.

- Colors

The colors used to identify the Orisha god of mischief are red and black or white and black.

Ibeji

Ibeji are a set of twin Orishas sacred to the Yoruba tradition. The word Ibeji roughly translates to two-born. Twins are thus considered to be sacred to the people of Yoruba. They have the highest rate of twin births as compared to the rest of the world. The Ibeji are considered one Orisha and are said to have one soul in two bodies. They are associated with joy, mischief, and glee.

- **Origin Story**

Oshun, the mother of Ibeji, was shunned by people when she gave birth to twins because twin births were supposedly unusual at that time. Only animals could give birth to multiple, identical offspring. So, the people labeled Oshun a witch and shunned her. Because of this, Oshun refused to accept Ibeji as her own offspring and threw them out of her house. Oya later adopted the Ibejis.

- **Personality**

Considered to be the protector of children, Ibeji Orisha is always represented as a baby or small child. Although depicted as this, Ibeji is a warrior in Yoruba history.

- **Colors**

Usually, red, white, and sometimes blue colors are associated with Ibeji.

- **Food and Offerings**

Food offerings for Ibeji are usually beans, sugarcane, pumpkin, ekuru, vegetables, red-palm oil, and cake.

Ọbàtálá

Ọbàtálá is known for creating the human body and the sky and is therefore also called the sky father. Rumored to be the oldest Orisha, Ọbàtálá comes among one of the white Gods of creativity. The word Ọbàtálá is broken and translated to Oba, which means king, and tala, which means undyed fabric. More commonly, Ọbàtálá is considered to be the father of all Orishas and mankind. Ọbàtálá is associated with wisdom, purity, peacefulness, and compassion.

- Origin Story

Ọbàtálá came down to earth from heaven to mold the bodies of the first humans. In addition to the primordial Ọbàtálá, his mortal counterpart was the founder and king of Ile-Ife. The Orisha Ọbàtálá hence originated as a mixture of the two.

- Personality

Ọbàtálá is described as a gentle and peace-loving Orisha associated with forgiveness, resurrection, honesty, and purpose. Also commonly known as the king of the white cloth, Ọbàtálá is said to be an extremely tranquil judge.

- Colors

The color associated with Ọbàtálá is pure white, representing the purity he brings.

- Food and Offerings

Food offerings made to Ọbàtálá are white in color to represent purity. These include rice, meringue, cocoa butter, and coconut.

Odùduwà

Odùduwà is considered one of the reigning ancestors among the kings of Yoruba. More commonly known as the Orisha of humans. His name roughly translates into the hero, the warrior, the father, and the leader of the Yoruba race. According to Yoruba tradition, Odùduwà was Olodumare's favorite Orisha, and he held an important role in the story of creation.

- Origin Story

Odùduwà was one of the deities involved in the task of developing the earth's crust. After Obatala got drunk on palm wine and was unable to develop the land, Odùduwà was sent to complete his task. The point on earth where he jumped from heaven and converted into land was named Ile-Ife, which is now considered the heart of Yorubaland.

• Personality

Odùduwà was a conquering warrior associated with creation, salvation, and power. He had no recognizable human form and is said to dwell deep in the darkness. Sometimes, he is referred to as the king of the dead in Yoruba tradition.

• Colors

Although Odùduwà is associated with death, his colors are white and opal.

Ògún

Ogun, also called the Orisha of iron, is known as the father of civilization in Yoruba mythology. He is said to be a protector of his people and a very just leader. Known for his creativity and intelligence, he invented the many tools humans needed for their survival. Otherwise, the earth would have remained a wilderness. He is also known for his strength and sacrifice. He supposedly cleared the path for his fellow Orisha to come to earth with his knives.

• Origin Story

Ogun's origin story tells how he ended up being the Orisha of iron. The Orisha and humans are said to have once existed together on land. Both of them leveled land to create more space to live. However, when the population increased, it became more and more difficult to find land and cultivate it. The tools used at that stage were made of wood, stone, or soft metal. One by one, all the Orisha tried to clear the land. However, none of them were able to succeed. This was when Ogun cleared the path with his iron knives. The other Orisha then made him a ruler in exchange for his knowledge about iron but later banned him. However, humans still remember and worship him to this day.

- **Personality**

There are two sides to the personality of Ogun; protective, fierce, and bloodthirsty versus creative, innovative, and intelligent. He can be the angriest warrior out of all Orisha at times while also showing a creative and calm side when designing his tools. He liked to hunt with his hand-crafted tools in densely forested areas.

- **Colors**

Being the Orisha of iron and war, the colors associated with Ogun are green, red, and black signifying the forest, fire, and war.

- **Food and Offerings**

Ogun prefers sacrificial offerings of catfish, alligator pepper, palm wine, roosters, red palm oil, and the like.

Okó

Oko is considered the farming and fertility deity among the Orishas. He is said to hold the secrets to farming and maintaining fertility in crops. He maintains the stability of life through his rotation of crops which provides humans with nutrition to survive. Oko is also the judge of Orishas and jumps to the defense of any female when an argument arises.

- **Origin Story**

Oko was given a piece of mechanical contraption by Ogun to help with his crops. It consisted of two oxen, which he became symbolized by. He was the first one to build a farm and cultivate the land to feed his family.

- **Personality**

Oko has a warm and harmonious personality. He is all about growth and the cultivation of life. Moreover, he is a trusted advisor for women and helps infertile women bear children.

- **Colors**

Oko is associated with the colors light blue and pink.

- **Food and Offerings**

Food offerings made to Oko can include all sorts of harvest food, dried meat, beans, yams, and slugs.

Osanyin

Osanyin is largely associated with plants, healing, and magic. He is a strong wizard, well respected for his magical abilities. He is the deity who has extensive knowledge of the medicinal purposes of herbs, roots, leaves, and plants. Many faith rituals in Yoruba involve Osanyin's plants and herbs.

- **Origin Story**

Osanyin was a crippled Orisha, missing one leg and one arm, and was blind in one eye. However, his brother Orunmila wanted Osanyin to feel better, so he asked Osanyin to pull out weeds from the crops early in the morning. When Orunmila returned the following evening, he found his brother crying in the field, having picked not a single weed out. When asked why Osanyin replied with the various healing abilities of different plants present there, his brother was astonished at the level of knowledge Osanyin had regarding plants. Since then, Osanyin has been declared the deity of plants, herbs, and healing.

- **Personality**

Osanyin loved nature and liked to collect knowledge about the various plants and herbs he found present in the forest. He has extensive healing abilities and is considered kind and humble.

- Colors

The various colors associated with Osanyin are green, yellow, black, red, and white.

- **Food and Offerings**

Typical food offerings for Osanyin are meat, nuts, chili, etc.

Oṣùmàrè

The name Oṣùmàrè roughly translates to rainbow, and that is exactly what Oṣùmàrè is associated with. Residing at the back of the mountains, Oṣùmàrè's duty is to fill the sky with beautiful colors to convey messages from the earth to heaven and vice versa. He is associated with unity and peace and symbolizes the balance between humans and Orisha.

- **Origin Story**

When the earth was created, the Orishas and divinities came into existence. Oṣùmàrè was ordered to signal a rainbow across the sky, indicating the creation of the universe was complete. Oṣùmàrè carries messages from Oluron, ruler of heaven to earth.

- **Personality**

Osùmàrè controls change, movement, and mobility. He is all about transformations and cyclic processes. His personality is very kind and giving. He loves the humans very much and showers them with blessings. He also controls rain and drought. He is also said to be the protector of children and controls the umbilical cord since it is considered the link between our world and that of our ancestors.

- **Colors**

The colors associated with Osùmàrè are white and silver. White is the color through which the different prism of rainbow colors is formed.

- **Food and Offerings**

Osùmàrè's favorite food is boiled white corn with coconut. He also likes rum.

Sàngó

Sàngó is one of the most powerful rulers in the Yoruba empire. Sàngó is also associated with thunder and lightning. Considered one of the most powerful and feared Orisha, he strikes anyone who offends him with lightning.

- **Origin Story**

In addition to the primordial existence of Sàngó, his earthly existence is also worth noting. He was the third Alaafin of Oyo and brought prosperity to the empire. His reign lasted seven years and was ended abruptly because his palace was destroyed by lightning.

- **Personality**

He was a violent and aggressive ruler, unlike his brother Ajaka. However, this violence came with commendable courage to fight many battles throughout his reign. Thus, he is worshiped with the strong beats of the Bata drum.

- **Colors**

The colors associated with Ṣàngó are mainly red and white. The bead pattern varies in groups of four and six, which are his sacred numbers.

- **Food and Offerings**

The sacred food associated with Ṣàngó is amala, a stew of okra mixed with palm oil and shrimp.

Chapter 6: How Ifa Divination Peeks into the Future

Since the beginning of time, divination has been an aspect of all cultural experiences and practice, in one way or another. This practice comes in numerous forms across the globe. It can be diagnostic, in the sense that it's used to detect illnesses or ailments, forecasting, implying that it's used to determine future events, and interventionist, so that practitioners use it to change the destinies of their clients. Some forms of divination that the Ancient Greece prophets practiced involved the belief that the practitioner had experienced direct contact with a supernatural entity. This is often known as inspirational divination. Other forms, however, which were practiced by Mongolian Shamans, Yoruba priests of divination, and African basket diviners, require a type of trained skill.

Divination Techniques

Many believe that you need both skill and inspiration to practice most forms of divination. The elements of nature are what shape divination activities. This explains why they are nature-based and can be carried out using natural materials like water, nuts, bones, and tea leaves. The use of cards and other man-made materials is also very common. There are also spontaneous forms of divination, which can include observing the behavior of birds. African people use many different types of divination, which often don't rely on using objects. For instance, Malian Doon diviners draw box-like shapes on the sandy soil, then arrange food, symbols, and sticks within them. They use words or invocations and call upon a fox to set the process in motion and reveal answers to their clients' questions. When the fox comes to eat, the objects in the box get moved around. The diviner receives his answers by reading the traces left by the animal.

Other African divination techniques rely on objects to get to the other realm. The Democratic Republic of Congo's Kuba uses *itombwa* or friction oracles carved by artists. These oracles are carved in the shape of elephants, crocodiles, wild pigs, and especially dogs. On very rare occasions, a human figure placed horizontally and over a four-legged animal is used. These oracles are used as a means of communication with the spirits of nature to aid in diagnosing the causes and cures of illnesses, the identification of malefactors, and eliminating other problems that may act as a threat to society.

The Popularity of the Yoruba Ifa Divination

The Yoruba Ifa divination, which will be explored in this chapter, is among the most well-known divination techniques. This is perhaps the result of the vast amount of research into the Yoruba, religion, and people. This heightened interest is perhaps due to the strong association between the Yoruba in Africa and the Americas. Plenty of the elements present in the Yoruba belief system have survived the passage of time; some have even been *reinvented*. This is because many of the enslaved people during the slave trades to be sent to the "New World" were Yoruba people brought from West Africa. Being pulled away from their people and home, the Yoruba insisted on keeping their traditions alive. Slave owners and missionaries took extreme measures to ensure that the African culture would be entirely stamped out. However, despite their efforts, the Yoruba always found a way to keep their beliefs alive. For this reason, many religious elements were maintained and still flourish in the Americas today. The preservation of Yoruba concepts, along with the renewed interest in traditional African religions, is exactly why you can find a Yoruba diviner in any of the United States' large cities.

Reading this chapter will help you learn the Ifa divination practice, how it works, and when it is used. We will describe what the 256 Odu are and how the sacred palm nuts and the divination chain are used. Finally, you'll also understand what a *Babalawo* is and how you can become one.

Ifa Divination

The Yoruba have various divination practices. However, they believed Ifa divination to be the most intricate and accurate of all their practices. This form of divination is related to the use of mathematics and a robust structure of oral tales and poems. Ifa is central to the Yoruba's culture, society, and religion. It is thought to incorporate a vital source of cosmology, belief system, and knowledge. The term *Ifa* points to both the Yoruba god of divination, also known as Orunmila, and the divination practice itself. The divination practice is common in many West African groups, especially the Fon people from the Republic of Benin.

One method known as the Ifa method of divination involves performing a full ritual where the diviner, a priest, the client, and the Yoruba people's cosmological and social order have to interact. This is the only way in which helpful answers can be found to the questions asked by clients. The Ifa divination practice occurs when a client asks for help from the order of supernatural beings with undetectable issues. Most clients tend to seek answers related to journeys, the nation's fate, such as a successor to the king, promising marriages, or illnesses. The greatest thing about Ifa is that it is open to everyone, which means that no problems are considered too complex, hard, irrelevant, or small when consulting Ifa. The Yoruba have high confidence and a deep belief in Ifa, which is why it governs the moral order and cosmology of the Yoruba. Ifa has been declared the deity source of knowledge of everything that exists in the universe. The deity is mentioned as an all-knowing storyteller and is the middleman between the people and the other gods and a historian. He is the deity of wisdom and intellect and the Yoruba's public relations handler. Also, Ifa takes on the role of the Yoruba all-powerful healer. For that, the deity is highly respected and valued among the members of society. When a client's ailment is assigned and determined by a diviner, the appropriate sacrifice is conducted, and healing occurs.

How It Works

The Ifa divination process occurs when a diviner is asked for consultation and casts the opele, or the divining chain, on a divining mat. The diviner may use sixteen palm nuts to come to a solution. The results of the divination process are known as the Signs or *Signature of Ifa*. Essentially, the results are usually one of 256 viable signs. The manipulation of the divining chain's 16 palm nuts results in a double tetragram, which is considered the result. The diviner then uses their finger to trace the *Signature of Ifa*. The diviner is also supposed to sprinkle *iyerosun,* a yellow divining powder, over the *Opon Ifa* or divining tray's surface, making the signs clearer. The diviner announces the results, and he chants. This process is also supposed to invoke the Signature of the Ifa deity, who delivers a message that the diviner should recite. The diviner should then clarify the message to their client and assign them the sacrifices they should conduct.

The 256 Odu

As you may recall, the Yoruba religion is founded upon scriptures of oral literature. These scriptures are known as the *Ifa Corpus* or the *Odu Ifa*. The Odu Ifa is a set of Ifa spiritual traditions, historical data, cultural information, and everlasting wisdom. This blend of knowledge has been put together through the centuries by using divination, interactions with the universe, and physical experiences and events. Diviners continue to enrich their knowledge and life journey by referring to this source of infinite wisdom.

Many followers refer to the *Odu Ifa* as the blueprint of life. This source is believed to act as a form of guidance for humanity. It allows humans to move positively toward manifesting their fates and making it through challenging periods in life. An accurate interpretation of the *Odu Ifa* can help answer questions and determine unknown outcomes.

The Yoruba oral tradition suggests that the 16 Odu were originally 16 divine prophets. Those heavenly entities supposedly came to Earth and made themselves known to the prophet of Ifa religion and wisdom, *Orunmila.* According to another oral tradition. Orula and Odudwa had 16 children together, considered symbols of the 16 vital Odu. These Odu Ifa signs are the basis of Ifa tradition and are where the other 240 Ifa signs come from.

The centuries' worth of wisdom and knowledge regarding spiritual enlightenment, moral philosophies, ethics, life experiences, sacrifices, rituals, etc., are represented by the Odu. This information is presented in the form of *ese,* meaning verse. Each Odu integrates information with two sides: the good and the bad. It includes instruction on how to manifest the good and guidance on how to curb and diminish negative, intrusive forces.

The 256 Odu Ifa is the entire set of Ifa Corpus, with the 16 previously mentioned Odu being its pillars. The basis of the Ifa religion is made up of 256 Odu in total. A practitioner must serve an intensive and rigorous apprenticeship to give an accurate reading. This process can take 15 to 30 years, and sometimes even more. This is because the diviners must memorize the entire collection of the Ifa verses.

Becoming a Babalawo

The Yoruba diviners are known as the Babalawo. Anyone who wants to become an Ifa priest, or a *Babalawo,* must be ready to dedicate their existence to Ifa and Olodumare. The term *Babalawo* can be translated into the *"Father of the Mysteries or Secrets of the Earth."* Becoming a Babalawo is the pursuit of a lifetime and is only suitable for individuals who wish to submit themselves to the practice and incorporate it into their lifestyles not only as a career but as a calling and lifestyle.

It is standard procedure to ask an individual who wishes to become an Ifa priest a set of questions designed to validate their motivation to become a priest. Traditionally, those who want to learn about Ifa for meat will receive an abundance of meat, those who wish to do it for money will get a lot of money, and people who wish to practice gaining many wives will get many wives. However, those who wish to become an Ifa priest in pursuit of the truth will gain all the riches in life, including the meat, money, and wives. While these questions may be a little dated, the principle behind them is that those who practice divination to seek the truth are better off than those who do it for personal gain or interest.

There are numerous procedures to be followed on the journey to becoming a *Babalawo*. If not completed under the guidance of a priest or master, the apprentice will never truly be a *Babalawo*. The first step includes the completion of the Ounje Oju Opele, or the food of Opele ritual. This ritual comprises numerous steps that must be completed in order. After eating the food of Opele, the master will open the 16 Odu Ifa with the Akaragba, which is made for the calabash that is used to conduct sacrifices to Esu, the apprentice, for five days. The Akaragba must be used when learning about Ifa and must be kept safe for life. Those who are fast learners may be exposed to the Odu more quickly. After the apprentice learns to open the Oju Odu Merindinlogun, they move on to the next step, divination. This is followed by learning how to receive answers to "yes" and "no" questions. In this step, the student learns about an Odu that helps with divination. Afterward, they learn how to make an ibo, characterized by aspects of good and bad. The master will teach the apprentice the elements of each and the differences between male and female readings. Then, the student will start learning about the Odu Ifa. They must memorize them too. This process may take a very long time, depending on the apprentice's memory.

After a while, the student will progress to learning how to make sacrifices and feed all the Orisha. The apprentice will also start learning about the elements of Ifa and the accompanying Odu Ifa, along with its negative and positive facets. The student must also learn how to create medicines for a wide array of ailments. All this information must be memorized well, as the student can't refer to notes or books for guidance. A person's initiation to Ifa doesn't mean that they've become a Babalawo. It simply means that their learning journey has started.

From the moment we were created, we have always used a wide array of methods in hopes of making sense of the world around us. Think of the I Ching of China, the tarot cards of Europe, and even the spider divination techniques of the Incans. African divination is no different from any of the others. It uses random objects and techniques to forge a connection with the spiritual realm and identify the causes and solutions to problems. Practitioners of divination are mentored by specialists and undergo training to become masters. Clients visit diviners who live elsewhere. This is because local diviners can use information that they heard about the client's work or family situations to connect the dots and give a reading. Meanwhile, visiting a stranger would force the diviner to rely solely on their methods of connecting with the spiritual realm.

Chapter 7: Honoring Your Ancestors

Ancestors play a critical role in the Yoruba religious system. They provide a link between what we can see and the invisible. This chapter discusses the significance of ancestors and the steps you can take to honor them. It also provides instructions on how to create an ancestor altar.

Significance of Ancestors

You can talk to the ancestors and ask for guidance and help when you need it. Since ancestors once lived as humans on earth, they better understand our needs, wants, and desires. However, this is a two-way street – you need to honor the lives of your ancestors if you want to get the help you need. Like any other religion in any other part of the world, ancestors are commemorated for their struggles, triumphs, and work they do for the living people. They drink what we drink, eat what we eat, do what we do, and go wherever we go. Therefore, we need to honor our ancestors to appreciate their presence in our lives.

Building an Ancestor Shrine

In the Yoruba religion, it is believed that everyone has an obligation and can communicate with their ancestors daily. If you want to communicate with your ancestor, you don't need any special knowledge or skills. Communicating with the ancestors is a simple gesture where you remember the departed when you make important decisions in life. The wisdom we get from our parents' folklore or oral tradition is enough to help us talk to the ancestors.

The most common method of communicating with the ancestors is through dreams. Taking part in festivals and other ancestor ceremonies which honor their existence in our lives is how you can get the information you are seeking. When honoring your ancestors, you should have a shrine, and there are different Yoruba methods you can consider building one. You should construct a shrine if you can access the lineage of your elders. Consult the ancestors for guidance when you gather the required things. Modifications and other elements can come later once your shrine is in place.

When you complete your shrine, you can communicate directly with your ancestors through activities like divination, visions, and other states of mental consciousness. You should get a bundle of nine sticks which you should tie with a red cloth. A priest with knowledge of Yoruba rites must identify the tree where you can collect the twigs. This bundle of sticks will be placed on your shrine, and this is where you'll present all your offerings, including food, drink, and animals.

Creating an Altar

As an alternative to a shrine, you can also build an altar where you'll perform your rituals to honor the ancestors. Find an area in your home or outside that you can use for prayer and meditation. You should put appropriate items on the altar and keep it clean. It is believed that dirt attracts evil spells and negative energy. You can use smoke to cleanse your altar. It is common in Yoruba tradition to find weeds with an aromatic scent and place them in a clay pot. Light the weeds to create smoke and make sure it reaches all the rooms if your altar is inside the house.

As you fan the smoke into each room of your house, say a prayer is asking the ancestors to remove negative energy from your home. The container you choose for this particular purpose should be reserved for ritual work only and keep it at your shrine. You can say the following prayer to appease the ancestors to remove negative elements.

"I pay homage to the spirits of the ancestors.

I am (state your name) the child of (mention your lineage).

I pay homage to the spirit of leaves.

Send away the spirit of death.

Send away illness.

Send away all gossip."

You say this prayer directly to the leaves. When you finish your prayer, breathe on the leaves, and say the word used to lock the prayer. The word also indicates that the invocation is over. Keep your thoughts focused on the intention of cleansing. It is crucial to have your altar in a neutral environment so that you'll be able to invite ancestors to your shrine. Emotional energy can linger in a room, which is why you should periodically clean the area to get rid of it.

Cleansing the altar should follow the same procedure you take when cleaning your body. The smoke should be fanned in the same direction. After performing the cleansing ritual, seal it with herbs and water. There are different types of herbs that can be used for locking in positive energy. Clearwater can be mixed with *efun or cascaria. Efun* is a white substance made from fossilized seashells. You can add cologne or other special types of fragrance to the water. Ideally, a scent you wear periodically. Put some fluids obtained from your body, like saliva or urine, into the water. This is an act of adding your presence to the seal. This will be a statement to the spirit realm to mark your invitation to your ancestors to enter.

You can use a traditional *Ifa* prayer to enhance the power of the water. Additionally, you need to say an enhancement prayer so you can include any other things you want. The following prayer will provide an ancestral invitation.

"I pay homage to the spirit of water

I am your child

Bring me

The good fortune of peace

The fortune of a stable home

Good fortune to my children

The good fortune of an abundance

The good fortune of long life

The good fortune of an ancestor shrine

The good fortune of the blessing brought by my higher self from the realm of the ancestors."

Say this prayer to the water. When you finish, sprinkle the water in all the places that the smoke has cleansed. When you are working on the sacred space, you should apply your conscious mind in everything you do. It is vital to welcome the ancestors to the altar as part of honoring them.

You also need to exclude ancestors who displayed violent or addictive behavior. The presence of such ancestors at your shrine can introduce similar influences, which will be a curse on your family. You need to identify the problems you don't want at your shrine. Once you identify the spirits who are welcome, you can start communicating with them directly to honor them. As your skills of communicating with the spirits develop, you can construct your ancestor altar. This should come after the cleansing ceremony.

An altar is a place where we remember the departed people who have joined the spiritual world. It's a place where we consider the wisdom of our lineage and determine how it will inform and guide us through different problems we may encounter. Your construction must be simple, and you should avoid complicated things. When you use a box, make sure you cover it with a white cloth and place a glass of water and a candle on top. These are basic elements that create human beings, representing the earth, fire, air, and water.

You can use the walls behind your altar to display the images of your relatives. By seeing a picture of your revered ancestor, you are reminded of how they solved different issues during their lifetime. Remembering is also a good practice since it inspires and resolves challenging issues we may encounter. Images of the ancestors constantly remind us of their contributions and how they continue to guide us.

We all come from diverse backgrounds and have encountered a variety of spiritual influences. Most people get into contact with these spiritual influences through reading different books like the Bible, Koran, I Ching, or Buddhist Sutra. You should combine these spiritual influences with Ifa to understand different worldviews.

You must light your candle on the altar and stand in front of it to honor your ancestors. The other thing you should do is to show your commitment to the altar you use for your daily prayers and meditation. You must develop self-discipline with regard to the way you use your altar.

For instance, you can commit to using your sacred space at least one day a week. Do not commit yourself to an agreement you cannot honor since this can cause distrust among your ancestors.

When you agree with your ancestors over how you'll communicate with them, you form a spiritual connection with them. Elements like cloth, water sources, candles, and pictures attract the spirit to the shrine. The prayers you say on your altar will cement the connection between you and the ancestors.

You should always turn to your sacred altar regardless of your situation to strengthen the flow of the currents. You should not only remember your altar when you are going through difficult times; *that can weaken the current of your prayer.* It should be charged regularly, so you must dedicate time to remembering your departed relatives daily. You also need to imagine how your role models can help solve different challenges you may encounter.

Ancestor Offering

Another great way of honoring your ancestors is to make food offerings to the altar. In Yoruba, this type of offering is called *adimu egun*. The purpose of making an offering is to create reciprocity where we ask the ancestors for guidance while we give them something in return. The ancestors eat and drink the same things as us, so offering them similar items is a great way of honoring them. Food offerings do not necessarily mean your ancestors are hungry, but it is just a gesture to show that you remember them.

In Yoruba tradition, you must present a small portion of food at the edge of your eating mate as a sign to honor your ancestors. You can also use a plate in front of your Egun altar to provide your food offering. The plate is a symbol of the body that is buried underneath the earth when the spirit rises to the other world. The food offering is traditional, and drinks often accompany it.

Traditional alcoholic beverages are often used in African traditions as part of the honoring exercise. Alternatively, you can also place a cup of coffee or tea on the altar to accompany your food offering in the plate.

You can also use flowers as direct offerings to the ancestors. You place them on the altar, and some people can also use cigars to honor their ancestors. The smoke is used to cleanse the place. Once you establish a communication link with the ancestors, they will tell you the things they want as offerings. Try to follow the instructions provided by the ancestors for guidance. Express gratitude and thank the ancestors when you finish presenting your offering.

You should feed your ancestors regularly to honor them for everything they do for you. This can go a long way in helping keep the ancestors close to your altar. In Africa, most people provide an offering of food before they drink anything. When you live in a foreign country, you must make a weekly offering. If you maintain a schedule, you'll not need to feed your ancestors regularly.

When you are not initiated, your ancestor shrine will provide an alternative system you can use for divination. These divination practices are based on Odu Ifa. The divination is usually directed at a particular spirit, and the spirit will bring messages from different sources. However, invocations meant to open divination are directed at a specific Orisa or Egun.

The ancestors form an integral part of our lives since they are ever-present in whatever we do. They eat and drink the same things, just like human beings. The ancestors provide us wisdom and guidance in different things we may need to achieve. However, to get what we want from our ancestors, we need to honor them to express our gratitude for their good work. We have discussed different methods we can consider honoring our ancestors. You need a shrine to perform any ritual directed to your ancestors, and you must decorate your sacred place with the right items. More importantly, there are certain prayers you should recite when you present an offering to your ancestors. Close each session with appropriate words to thank them.

Chapter 8: Yoruba Worship Calendar and Holy Days

Just like the Yoruba people have their own language, they have their own calendar and holy days as well. The Yoruba calendar is called KÓJÓDÁ, which means "may the day be clearly foreseen." Their year begins on June the 3rd of the Gregorian calendar and ends on June the 2nd of the next year. The year 2022 AD is the 10,064th Yoruba year.

The Yoruba calendar has 12 months in its year like the Georgian calendar, but this is where the similarities end. The weeks are longer in the Yoruba calendar as there are 91 weeks, but the days are shorter with only four days a week. This didn't last long, though, as they have changed their calendar to correspond with the Georgian calendar. Now there are four weeks a month and each week is seven days. They use this calendar for a business, while the older version is dedicated to the Orishas.

The Days of the Yoruba Calendar

The four days in the traditional Yoruba calendar are dedicated to different Orishas:

- **Day 1** is dedicated to Orisha Obatala, the father of the sky, Sopona (god of smallpox), Iyami Aje (which means respect), and Egungun (Yoruba masquerade)

- **Day 2** is dedicated to Orunmila, the Orisha of knowledge and wisdom, Esu (trickster god), and Ọṣun, the Orisha of Wisdom

- **Day 3** is dedicated to Ogun, the Orisha of iron and metal, and Oshoshi, the Orisha of hunting

- **Day 4** is dedicated to Sango, the Orisha of lightning, and Oya, his wife, and the Orisha of the weather

The seven days of the updated version that reconciles with the Gregorian calendar are:

Days in English	Days in Yoruba
Sunday	Ọjọ́-Àìkú, the day of immortality
Monday	Ọjọ́-Ajé, the day of economic enterprise
Tuesday	Ọjọ́-Ìṣégun, the day of victory
Wednesday	Ọjọ́-rú, the day of confusion and disruption
Thursday	Ojọ́-Bò, the day of arrival
Friday	Ojó-Ẹ̀tì, the day of postponement and delay
Saturday	Ọjọ́-Àbámẹ́ta, the day of the three suggestions

The Months of the Yoruba Calendar

June

The first month in the Yoruba calendar is Òkùdú which is June in the Gregorian calendar. The third day of the Òkùdú is the Yoruba new year which is celebrated the same way the rest of the world celebrates the New Year with music, singing, and dancing. There are several Orishas who are celebrated and venerated during this month.

- **Oshosi**, the Orisha of hunting, is celebrated on June 6th

- **Eleguá**, the Orisha of roads, is celebrated on June 13th

- **Oṣun**, the guardian of Ọrunmila and the Orisha of Wisdom, is celebrated on June 24th

- **Oggún**, the Orisha of iron is celebrated on June 29th

July

The second month in the Yoruba calendar is Agẹmọ. There are three Orishas who are celebrated in Agẹmọ.

- **Aggayú Solá**, the Orisha of volcanoes, is celebrated on July 25th

- **Oke**, the Orisha of the mountains, is celebrated on July 25th

- **Nana Buruku**, the Supreme Goddess, is celebrated on July 26th

August

The third month is named after the Orisha of iron, Ogun. There are two festivals that are usually celebrated this month; the Osun-Osogbo and the Sango festival.

The Osun-Osogbo festival takes place in Osun State in Nigeria every year. The festival celebrates Osun, the river Orisha, and it lasts for two weeks. Since 2005, the celebrations have taken place at a sacred forest that has the same name as the festival. The people of the town of Osogbo consider August to be the time when they can reunite with the culture of their ancestors, cleanse their city, and celebrate.

Various interesting activities take place in this city, like Iwo Popo, which is a traditional cleansing of their town. Another activity is lighting a 500-year-old 16-point lamp called Ina Oloju Merindinlogun, which lasts for three days. The last activity is the

Ibroriade, where they collect the crowns of their city's previous kings. Four people usually lead this festival; the sitting Osogbo king, a group of priestesses, the Yeye Osun, and the Arugba, who is a chosen virgin woman. This festival attracts people from all over the world, like tourists and Osun worshippers.

Now we are going to talk about the Sango festival, which takes place every year at the palace of Oyo's ruler. This place honors the god of thunder and iron, Sango. According to legends, Sango was the one who founded the Oyo state boundaries. The festival lasts for a week, and thousands of people from all over the world come to enjoy the celebrations. The festival is considered a tourism and cultural event that UNESCO recognizes. It is also celebrated in many other countries.

In 2013, the Oyo government changed the name of the Sango festival to the World Sango festival.

September

This month is called the Ọwẹ́wẹ̀ in the Yoruba calendar. There are four Orishas that are celebrated and venerated during this month.

- **Yemaya**, the Orisha of the surface of the ocean, is celebrated on September 7th

- **Oshun**, the Orisha river, is celebrated on September 8th

- **Obàtálá**, the creator of human beings and the father of the sky, is celebrated on September t 24th

- **Ibeyis**, the protective twin's Orisha, is celebrated on September 26th

One of the festivals during September is the Olojo festival. It is usually celebrated in Ife town in Osun, and it celebrates Ogun, the Orisha of iron. The people of Yoruba consider Ife to be their city of origin. According to the legends of Yoruba, Ogun is Oduduwa, the creator, first son. The Yoruba people believe they descended from Oduduwa. The word Olojo means "owner of the day," and it is believed that the creator has blessed this day. The Ife king, the Ooni, is usually secluded for a few days before appearing in public on this special day wearing the Are crown, which is the king's crown.

On the day of the festival, the king visits various shrines where he prays for Nigeria and the Yoruba lands to live in peace. This festival celebrates the unification of the people of Yoruba, which is why they hold it in very high esteem.

Another festival celebrated in September is the Igogo festival. This festival is usually celebrated in Owo, an ancient city in Ondo State. Once upon a time, the ruler of Owo was Olowo Rerengejen; he married Orosen, a goddess who became a queen and is honored every year in the Igogo festival.

The Igogo festival is celebrated for 17 days. The celebrations are quite unique and interesting. Since they are honoring a Goddess and a queen, the Owo king and his high chiefs all dress in women's clothes – like gowns. People also celebrate new yams during this festival, commemorating culture and life. It also marks the beginning and end of the farming season.

October

October is called Ọ̀wàrà in the Yoruba culture. There are three Orishas who are celebrated and revered during this month.

- **Orula**, the protector of divination, is celebrated on October 4th

- **Oya**, the mistress of the rainbow, is celebrated on October 15th

- **Inle**, the god of health, is celebrated on October 24th

November

This month is called Bélú. There aren't any Yoruba celebrations or festivals that take place in November.

December

December is called Ọ̀pẹ́. There are two Orishas celebrated and venerated during this month.

- **Shango**, the Orisha of lighting, is celebrated on December 4th

- **Babalú Aye**, the healing Orisha, is celebrated on December 17th

January

The first month in the Gregorian calendar is called Ṣẹ́rẹ́ in the Yoruba language. There are two Orishas celebrated during this month.

- **Eleguá**, the Orisha of roads, is celebrated on January 6th

- **Osain**, the Orisha of nature, is celebrated on January 17th

February

This month is called Èrèlè in the Yoruba calendar, and there is only one Orisha celebrated during this month.

- **Oya**, the Orisha of the weather is celebrated on February 2nd

The Eyo festival is the only one celebrated in February and is one of the most popular festivals in the Yoruba culture. It takes place every year in Lagos state. During the celebrations, costumed dancers called *Eyo* to come out to perform. *Eyo* means the tall Eyo masquerades, and an interesting fact about this celebration is that these masquerades only allow *tall people* to participate. There are certain rules to this festival; for instance, no one is allowed to wear any footwear, and a popular Yorubian hairstyle known as Suku is prohibited. However, the festival had a very different beginning; it was held to bid farewell to a departed Lagos king and welcome a new one.

There aren't as many followers of the Yoruba religions as there used to be because many followers have converted to Christianity or Islam. However, the Eyo festival is more popular than ever and is considered a huge tourist attraction. One of the reasons behind Eyo's popularity is the masquerade dancers that attract tourists worldwide. It is no wonder why the Lagos government holds this festival in very high regard. Since it attracts tourists from all over the world, this festival help boosts the state's economy, and small businesses benefit so much from it as well.

March

March is called Ẹrẹ̀nà in the Yoruba language. There aren't any Orisha celebrations or Yoruba festivals during this month.

April

April is called the Ìgbé, and only one Orisha is venerated in this month.

- **Yewa**, the Orisha of virginity, is celebrated on April 27th

There is only one festival celebrated in April: the Lagos Black Heritage Festival. It is one of the biggest and most important festivals, and it takes place in Lagos State. It is an annual colorful folk festival.

The African culture has a very rich history, and there is no denying that the African people are very proud of their heritage. This is obvious in the celebrations that take place at the Lagos Black Heritage Festival. It is a day when the Nigerian people proudly show the world their diverse culture. They use different events and entertaining activities to showcase their heritage to the world. They dance, play music, perform, display photos, and do many other festive activities. Additionally, the Lagos Island troops dress up in beautiful costumes and walk around town. It is no wonder it is considered one of the biggest Yoruba celebrations.

May

The last month in the Yoruba calendar is Ẹ̀bìbì. There are two Orishas celebrated in May.

- **Oko**, the Orisha of farming is celebrated on May 15th

- **Oba**, the Orisha of the rivers, is celebrated on May 22nd

The people of Yoruba celebrate the Oro festival in May. Unlike the other festivals usually celebrated in one town or state, this festival takes place in all the Yoruba towns in Nigeria. It is an annual festival with a very unique rule: Only certain people are allowed to participate in the festivities; they must be men or boys, and their fathers must be natives. So, what do the rest of the town's residents do during the festival? According to the rules, all women and non-natives must stay in their homes.

This ancient rule considers it taboo for anyone other than the male paternal natives to see Oro. Since this festival occurs in different towns, you'll find that each one has its own celebrations and traditions. In addition to being an annual festival, the Oro festival is also held when a Yoruba king passes away.

The last festival that we will discuss in this chapter is the Ojude Oba festival which doesn't occur in a specific month. It takes place three days after Eid Al Kabir, or as it is also called Eid Al Adha, a Muslim holiday honoring Ibrahim's willingness to sacrifice his son Ismael.

The Ojude Oba is another annual festival that takes place in Ijebu Ode in Ogun state. There are various activities that take place during this festival, and their purpose is to showcase their history with various entertaining events that focus on their legends and diversity. One of the most important events that take place during this festival is showing allegiance to the king. Wherever the town's natives reside in the country, they must travel to the town's king to show their respect. This festival is very popular since thousands of people attend it every year from all over the country. In addition to these festivals, the people of Nigeria also celebrate traditional holidays like Christmas, New Year, Easter, and two of the most popular Muslim holidays, Eid El Fitr and Eid El Adha.

The Yoruba culture is rich in its language, religion, and legends, and its festivals are as colorful and reflect its magic. The Yoruba people still hold on to their ancient traditions, which they proudly showcase during their festivals. Although these celebrations are all interesting with fascinating history, they are also a huge tourist attraction and boost the country's economy. While customs and traditions have become a thing of the past in many cultures, it is refreshing to see how the people of Yoruba keep theirs alive by celebrating their gods, Orishas, history, and heritage every year. One can understand why the rest of the world is still curious and fascinated with the culture of Yoruba.

Chapter 9: Yoruba Spells, Rituals, and Baths

As the title implies, this chapter contains several simple Yoruba spells, rituals, and baths suitable for beginner Yoruba practitioners. They can offer you protection, guidance, prosperity, and much more. Not only that but most of them can also be altered to suit anyone's individual needs and preferences or invoke a different Orisha if needed. Feel free to use them as they are or add your own spin on them by centering them more on your own specific beliefs.

Seven-Day Candle Ritual for Obatala

Calling on Obatala can be helpful when you need to eliminate negativity from your life or communicate your negative feelings towards the outside world. Using a white, Seven-day candle will ensure you acquire purity in mind and body. The addition of other white food will appease Obatala, so he lends you the ashe you need to obtain your goals.

You'll need:

- A piece of white cotton yarn
- Cascarilla – fresh or dry
- Yams
- Coconut shavings
- Milk
- Rice
- A white, Seven-day candle
- A representation of Obatala

Instructions:

1. Organize your altar or sacred space by clearing up anything you won't need for this ritual.

2. Place the white candle and a symbol representing Obatala on your altar.

3. Prepare the white food – rice, milk, coconut, yams – all in separate bowls and place those on the altar as well.

4. If you are using fresh or whole dried cascarilla, tie the plant in a bunch with a piece of white cotton yarn.

5. If you are using chopped dry leaves, spread them around the candle and tie the yarn around the bottom of the candle.

6. When you are ready, light the candle, close your eyes and prepare to call on Obatala.

Then, recite the following spell:

"Oh, great Obatala, please lend me your power,

Send me patience and knowledge.

May I be strong and wise,

So I can pursue my passions.

Help me stay fair and caring,

To treat others with great integrity."

While traditionally, the candle was intended to be left burning seven days and nights, this is not recommended primarily due to safety concerns. And even if you had a way to keep the candle safe at all times, the spell works only if you keep your mind focused on it. So, instead of worrying about potentially burning down your house (which alone will derail your thoughts from channeling your energy towards the spell), you should opt to burn the candle for regular periods of time over seven days. Whenever you have a little time during the day, light the candle, and recite the spell. When you are finished, snuff it out and go about your day, and when you can, relight it once again until it burns out. In addition, the food is supposed to be served raw, but Obatala will also accept your offering if you prepare a dish from all-white food sources.

Fertility Ritual

This traditional Yoruba ritual has been used by young women who want to conceive a child. Apart from this, Oshun may grant you fertility in many other aspects of life, such as art, work, and even cultivating relationships. The colors and seeds of the pumpkin symbolize the power of nature's fertility.

You'll need:

- 1 pumpkin
- 1 yellow candle
- 1 pencil
- 1 brown paper bag
- A representation of the goddess

Instructions:

1. Place the yellow candle in front of the representation of Oshun on your altar and light it.

2. Close your eyes and focus on manifesting your wishes. Saying them out loud often helps.

3. Open your eyes and carve a round opening in the top of the pumpkin.

4. Take the pencil, and write your wishes down on a piece of the paper bag.

5. Place the piece of paper inside the pumpkin, then pour candle wax on top of it.

6. After ensuring the pumpkin has been sealed with the wax, place it over your stomach, repeating your wishes.

7. When you feel your wishes have been heard, take the pumpkin to the nearest water source, and offer it to Oshun.

You may leave the candle burning for a short period after the ritual is completed, but if you leave it unattended, it's best to snuff it out. You can relight the candle any time you want to during the next five days.

A Prosperity Offering

There are several Orishas associated with prosperity. You can choose to invoke the one whose ashe you need the most according to the area of life you want to prosper in. For example, Oshun may grant you spiritual wealth while Olokun will provide material prosperity.

You'll need:

- 5 oranges
- 1 yellow candle
- 1 white plate
- Cinnamon
- Honey
- A representation of an Orisha

Instructions:

1. Place the yellow candle in front of the representation of the Orisha on your altar and light it.

2. Recite your wish out loud to make sure Orisha can hear you.

3. Put the oranges on a white plate and drizzle them with honey.

4. Sprinkle some cinnamon on top of the oranges as well.

5. Leave the oranges and the topping in front of the Orisha beside the candle for five days.

6. When the five days are up, you may throve or put away the candle and dispose of the offering too.

As with the previous ritual, the candle shouldn't be continuously burning for five days. Feel free to blow it out anytime you leave it and light it again when you can supervise it once again. Make sure to use fresh oranges that can stay safely at room temperature until the ritual is completed.

An Offering for Olokun

Offerings are typically made to Olokun around the time of the traditional harvest celebrations. However, they can also be made on any other occasional date throughout the year for different purposes. Regardless of the date, the offering is best performed in the open air so Olokun will witness the symbolic use of the items and know she is needed. You can incorporate this prayer into your regular practice, and you'll be blessed with Olokun`s protection and guidance.

You'll need:

- A representation of Olokun
- A white handkerchief
- Yemaya incense powder
- Charcoal
- Cowrie shells
- Fruit, grains, meat, and other offerings of your choice

Instructions:

1. Spread the white handkerchief on your altar and place the representation of Olokun on top of it.

2. Put the charcoal in a small bowl and pour some incense powder over it.

3. Light the incense, place the shells in a basket, and then make the offering.

4. Light the candle and say the following prayer:

"I praise the queen of the vast waters.

I praise the queen of the waters beyond understanding.

Oh, queen of the Ocean, I will honor you as long as there is water on the Earth.

Let there be calmness in the waters, so they bring peace to my soul.

I respect the ancient ruler of the water kingdom. Ashé, ashé. "

5. Relax your mind by focusing on the candle's flame or closing your eyes and meditating for a couple of minutes.

6. Work on manifesting your wishes until the incense burns out, then thank Olokun for the blessing she may bestow on you.

The Yemaya powder can be substituted for an incense powder of your choice. Your shell basket can also contain different types of shells, such as seashells – to evoke the queen of the water kingdom. If you offer meat, use only the part of an animal you have prepared to eat, as live animal sacrifices aren't recommended.

Ritual Love Bath

While Oshun is the female Orisha typically associated with love, others can help you make your wishes come true in matters of the heart. The white candle will ensure you see clearly, so you don't miss the person intended for you. The use of your favorite perfume will allow the initial attraction to happen.

You'll need:

- 5 sunflowers
- 1 white candle
- 1 bowl
- A representation of the goddess
- Honey
- Cinnamon
- Your favorite perfume

Instructions:

1. Place the white candle in front of the Orisha on your altar and light it.

2. Tell the Orisha about your wish to find love, preferably by saying it out loud.

3. Remove the petals of the sunflower, and place them in a bowl.

4. Drizzle the petals with honey, sprinkle them with cinnamon, and add a few spritzes of your favorite perfume to them.

5. Pour some water on top of the ingredients in the bowl.

6. Take a shower or a bath, and pour the contents of the bowl over your body. Start from your neck, and move towards your feet.

7. Close your eyes and repeat your wishes once again.

Once again, the candle should be lit for shorter or longer periods of supervised time for five consecutive days. However, the bath ritual itself is only to be repeated once every two to three weeks to leave enough time for love to come into your life.

Sour Bath

This bath aims to acknowledge that while your current life experiences are bitter ones, they can be overturned. Immersing yourself in a sour bath allows you to recognize the negativity around you and change things to work more in your favor. The bitter herbs help with seeing that you aren't the only one with negative experiences. The seven drops of ammonia represent the seven evil forces in Yoruba cultures.

You'll need:

- A pair of tea light candles

- Flowers with red or purple petals

- Fresh or dried bitter herbs, such as yarrow, stinging nettle, horehound, dandelion, and wormwood,

- A half-cup of vinegar – white, red, or apple cider

- Seven drops of ammonia

- An empty cup

Instructions:

1. Around sunset, fill up your bathtub with hot water. Make sure to adjust the temperature to your usual preferences.

2. While the bathtub fills, place the tea light candles around its rim and light them.

3. When the tub has been filled to the desired level, turn off all the electric lights in the bathroom.

4. Toss all the ingredients into the water, then enter the tub between two candles placed opposite each other.

5. Immerse yourself in the water, inhale the bitter scent of the herbs, and focus on the aspects of your life you want to change.

6. You may also pray to the Orishas you use as a guide and ask for their assistance in resolving your problems.

7. Occasional, you should immerse yourself completely in the water. The aim is to spend a total of seven minutes with your head underwater during the course of the bath.

8. Once you feel the water has begun to cool off, you should exit the tub through the gap between the same candle you have entered.

9. Start draining the water – but before it disappears, scoop some of it into the cup along with the ingredients.

10. Don't towel dry unless it's absolutely necessary – let yourself dry naturally instead so the effect of the herbs can soak into your skin.

11. Once you are dry, put on some dark clothes, and take the cup with the bathwater outside.

12. Stand facing west, and hold the cup over your head while saying:

> *"Supreme God who knows and sees all, I have given the Orisha their due. I now declare their hold on me strong. As I cast this water where it's needed, so do I cast out all my problems from my head and life. Ashé, ashé!"*

13. Toss out the water from the cup, head back indoors, and spend some time recouping your strength.

14. Make sure you drink lots of room temperature water so you can replenish the fluids you have lost while soaking in hot water.

This bath should be taken once a week, and it's even easier to incorporate into your regular beauty and healthcare practice than the previous one. Once again, if you want to avoid clogging up your drain while taking this bath, place the herbs into tea bags or organza bags. After your bath, you can spend the time with your normal health care regime, applying shea butter or other natural moisturizing agents, journaling, or meditating. You may also add prayers of gratitude to the Orishas or a deity of your choice. To maximize the ritual's therapeutic effects and ensure a restful sleep, avoid watching TV or using other electronic devices after your bath.

Sweet Bath

While the sour bath allows you to relieve your body of toxins and negative energy at sunset, the sweet one has the purpose of purifying and energizing you at sunrise. The ingredients such as milk, eggs, and honey will nourish your body and revitalize your mind anytime you feel the need for a little pampering.

You'll need:

- A pair of tea light candles

- Flowers with all-white petals such as lilies, roses, daisies, or white chrysanthemums

- Five different fresh or dried healing herbs such as rue, allspice, comfrey, angelica, and hyssop

- A small bottle or jar of honey

- 3 cups of milk

- Powdered cinnamon

- Powdered nutmeg and whole nutmegs

- 1 raw egg

- Your favorite perfume

- An empty cup

- Cocoa butter or shea butter – optional

Instructions:

1. Around sunrise, fill up your bathtub with hot water. Make sure to adjust the temperature to your usual preferences.

2. While the bathtub fills, place the tea light candles around its rim and light them.

3. When the tub has been filled to the desired level, turn off all the electric lights in the bathroom.

4. Crack the egg and toss it in the water. Don't worry if it starts to cook a little bit.

5. Throw on the flowers, herbs, cinnamon, and nutmeg, then follow it with the milk and the honey.

6. Finally, add a few drops of your favorite cologne to the water, then enter it through the gap between two candles as instructed in the previous ritual.

7. Immersing yourself in the water, and inhaling the sweet scent of the ingredients, focus on the good things that are already in your life. Think about good experiences that way for you on that day and be open to them.

8. You may also express your gratitude to the Orishas for the blessing you may receive on that day.

9. Make sure to immerse yourself fully for a total of final times during your bath.

10. Once you feel the water has begun to cool off, you should exit the tub through the gap between the same candle you have entered.

11. Start draining the water - but before it disappears, scoop some of it into the cup along with the ingredients.

12. Don't towel dry unless it's absolutely necessary - let yourself dry naturally instead so the effect of the herbs can soak into your skin.

13. Once you are dry, put on some light-colored clothes, and take the cup with the bathwater outside.

14. Stand facing east, and hold the cup over your head while saying:

> *"Supreme God who knows and sees all, I welcome with open arms all the beautiful things in life that are waiting for me on my journey! As I cast this water where it's needed, may it serve as an*

invitation for Oshun so she can bless me with health, love, prosperity, and happiness! Ashé, ashé!"

15. Toss out the water, head back inside and get ready to welcome the blessings you've invoked.

This bath should be taken once a week, like the previous one incorporated into your regular beauty and healthcare practice. Once again, if you want to avoid clogging up your drain while taking this bath, place the herbs into tea bags or organza bags. While you may not have time to meditate, journey, or perform any other self-care routine before heading out for the day, it's good to avoid using technology and stressful situations right after your bath.

Chapter 10: How Yoruba Influenced Santeria and Others

The Yoruba religion has significantly impacted the new world African diaspora, and it has led to the emergence of belief systems in countries such as Cuba (Santería/ Lucumí, Palo) and Brazil (Umbanda, Candomblé). It also connects with other less-known religions like Haiti (Vodou) and New Orleans (Voodoo/Voudou). This chapter explains how Yoruba religion has managed to influence these African diaspora religions. It also provides details about the similarities and differences between Yoruba and other religions.

Santería

Santeria was brought to Cuba by people from Yoruban countries in West Africa. These individuals were enslaved in the 19th century, but they managed to preserve their religion against the odds. Santeria is a Spanish name that means "The Way of the Saints" and is also known as La Regla de Ocha, meaning "The Order of the Orishas." La Religion Lucumi refers to "The Odu of Lucumi," and is the most popular name associated with religious traditions with origins from Africa and later developed in Cuba and spread to Latin America and the United States.

Santeria is mainly concerned about developing relationships through divination, initiation, sacrifice, and mediumship between the practitioners of the tradition and orisha deities. The main role of deities is to provide wisdom, success, guidance, and protection to the practitioners of the religion during difficult times. A trained priest in the Ifa oracle interprets and provides answers to the questions asked by the devotees. Offerings are presented during ceremonial exchanges, and this practice has since spread to Cuba and other Latin American countries.

Cuba is one of the few countries that received the greatest number of enslaved people from diverse African groups. During the slave trade, more than 700,000 people were enslaved from western Africa – and their final destination was Cuba. Due to the size of the African slaves, their religion of Yoruba continued to thrive even when the slave trade was abolished. The deities with Yoruba origins from Nigeria, Benin, and Togo are called Oricha or Orishas in Spanish. In Cuba and Haiti, the West African deities were paired with Roman Catholic saints, and the religious practice became known as Santeria, referring to "the way of the saints."

Many people are turning against this word since it undermines their religion and the legacy they inherited from their ancestors. Others within the Afro-Caribbean tradition refer to it as La Regla de Lukumi or "the order of Lukumi." Lukumi refers to "my friend," and it comes from the Yoruba greeting.

Following the outbreak of the Cuban revolution in the twentieth century, more than one million Cubans migrated to other cities in the United States. Most people with Yoruban roots moved to Miami and New York, and they later spread their religion to other places. The religion also spread to other cultures like Latinos, African Americans, and even the whites. Many people consulted orishas in the US.

The Cuban immigrants brought Ocha to the US characterized by selling herbs, religious articles, images of the tradition, and candles. While there is no visible public infrastructure, it is believed that between 250,000 and one million people practice this new religion brought by the diasporas in their home temples.

The Orisha tradition has received recognition in different parts of the United States. For example, in 1993, the US Supreme Court allowed the orisha devotees to use animal sacrifices as part of their rites in the case of *Church of the Lukumi Babalu Aye v. City of*

Hialeah. Orisha tradition is also portrayed through music, paintings, art, literature, and sculpting. It is likely to continue growing to become a renowned religion across the globe.

Candomblé

Candomblé, like other Afro-Caribbean religions, was brought to Brazil by African slaves between 1549 and 1888. When it emerged in Brazil, it exhibited the characteristics of African cultures, such as Yoruba and other traditions practiced by the Bantu and Fon. Despite being criminalized by other governments and banned by the Catholic Church, the religion thrived for about four centuries. Today, it is an established religion with followers from various social classes and several temples.

About two million Brazilians believe in Candomble religions. Elements like Candomble rituals, deities, and holidays are recognized as part of Brazilian folklore. Candomble refers to a dance meant to honor the gods. Music and dance often accompany many ceremonies and rituals. Most of these traditions are passed orally. Candomblé is practiced by more than two million people in different countries across the globe.

The Candomblé tradition worships the same deities as the Yoruba religion, and it also emphasizes that there is only one supreme creator known as Oludumaré. The intermediaries between the Oludumaré and people are known as orixas. There are also those who function as spirits, and they serve Oludumaré. All individuals are believed to originate from orixa and represent certain foods, colors, and other elements of nature. In Brazil, the spirits that are not deemed as deities are called "Baba Egum." When the devotees are performing a ritual, a priest will dress like the ancestor they want to summon. The women should be part of every ceremony since they will perform dances throughout the ceremony.

Sacred services are usually done in a temple, and some people practice the rituals in sacred places in their homes. Many people were compelled to convert to Catholicism once shipped from West Africa. This led to the protection of the Candomblé religion, which has roots in Yoruba. Candomblé was later condemned since it conflicted with the Catholic religion.

Umbanda

Umbanda is a religion born in Southern Brazil, and it combines Brazilian religion with African traditions, spiritism, and Catholicism. Being exposed to several different religions, such as Yoruba and Catholicism, led to the formation of a new syncretic religion.

Umbanda's formation was quite slow in the 19th century and was later officially recognized in Rio de Janeiro during the 20th century. It was found by Zélio Fernandino de Moraes who was a psychic. He was mainly influenced by spiritualist teachings that led him to create this Umbanda religion. According to the doctrine of spiritism, the souls of all the living things are immortal. The spirits of the dead can assist the living with worldly problems. Umbanda became more prominent in Brazil around the 1930s. This religious system acquired more structural elements from other religions like Yoruba and Catholicism.

There are several mainstream beliefs though there is no uniformity concerning Umbanda religion. Worship is usually done in backyard temples, and this is where many people gathered in the early days. The Umbanda religion's supreme deity is Zambi or Olorun. The orixas are the divine gods that reflect a connection between Zambi and humans. Each Oricha represents different things like justice, love, or protection.

Vodou

Vodou (or Vodoun) is a religion with traceable roots in African traditions which date back to about 6,000 years. Slaves forcibly shipped from Africa brought this religion to Haiti and other islands found in the West Indies. Vodou's birth resulted from a mixture of different cultures like the African religions and Catholic principles in Haiti. A massive number of Africans were transported to the island as slaves, but their large numbers helped them maintain their religion.

Just like the Yoruba cosmology, Voudou's origins also speak of one supreme god known as the Bondye. The believers of this god are convinced that he is the one who created the universe and is also responsible for overseeing human life. Some intermediaries act between this god and the devotees. These can be ancestors or Iwa who are equivalent to Orishas. The Iwa can be divided into two categories based on the African religion, and the following are the most significant.

- **Rada Iwa** - These are benevolent, wise, and helpful spirits gifted with perfume and candy, and they have their origins in Nigeria.

- **Petwa Iwa** - These spirits are malevolent and aggressive, and they are gifted with rum, gunpowder, and firecrackers. They have Congo origins.

Since the Vodou combines various ethnic traits and religious traditions, Iwa was also combined with a Catholic Saint and included the following associations:

- **Damballa/Saint Patrick** - Was perceived as a grandfather figure and also associated with snakes

- **Ogou/Saint George** - A warrior deity who presided over politics, war, and fire.

- **Baron Samedi** – This was the Iwa for the dead, resurrection, and sex. He is known for debauchery and obscenity.

- **Papa Legba/Saint Peter** – The deity is known for being deceptive and persuasive.

- **Erzulie Dantor** – Was later known as the mother of all Haitians and a protector of children.

The Vodou Religion and Haitian Revolution

Between 1791 1ne 1804, the enslaved Africans began to challenge the white plantation owners in Haiti. The slaves were also reorganizing themselves, and the following are some of the things that occurred.

- There were about 250 000 slaves from Africa in the colony

- Only 25 000 white settlers ruled the slaves

- Boukman and Mandal, two prominent Vodou priests and slaves, became the face of the early revolution.

- Vodou was not recorded in text; therefore, masters could not determine what was being planned. Religion was used as a group conscience.

- Vodou ceremonies, such as sacrifices, were performed, and it was believed that religion played a role in the ensuing victory.

- The French were overthrown in 1804, allowing Haiti to become the first colony ruled by slaves.

- Haiti was economically isolated to avoid more revolts, and the Catholic clergy fled and resurfaced around 196, which led to the mixture of the Vodou religion and Catholic motifs without controversy.

- The presence of Catholicism in Haiti led to the persecution of Vodou followers. They were believed to use superstition and other satanic rituals such as cannibalism. All the persecutions were carried out under the 1896 Anti-Superstition Campaign.

- While the persecution later ceased, Vodou is still seen as a sign of backward digression in other parts of the world.

Vodou Rituals and Practices

Vodou rituals are performed in the temple, also known as an ounfo. People will draw veves on the temple walls, and they relate to a particular Iwa.

- When rituals are in progress, an Iwa will possess other devotees. The Iwa should be of the opposite sex.

- Trances can last several hours, and the affected person will not remember anything after coming out of the trance

- Vodou practitioners are called Vodouisants, and the priests are known as mambos and oungans. They assisted people through divination in different problems.

- Vodou culture is associated with negative perceptions like reanimating the dead into zombies. However, this has not been proved anywhere.

After the Haitian revolution, many refugees from the colony migrated to the United States of America to find a new life for themselves. In doing so, they carried their cultural and religious traditions. Vodou and other American religions have been blended, and the Vodou culture is practiced in different areas in the US, such as New Orleans. The increased number of black refugees traveling to the US in the 19th century led to an increase in the Vodou belief system in Louisiana and other Southern states.

Afro-Caribbean and Vodou now include other components of Christianity and American religion. Christian ministers around New Orleans now include some of the Vodou traditions in their sermons since this religion is becoming popular. The leaders of this religion, also known as Voodoo Kings and Queens, were renowned as political figures.

For example, Dr. John, known as Bayou John, is still a famous Voodoo king of New Orleans today. After being born in Senegal, John Bayaou was taken to Cuba as a slave. He settled in New Orleans and was an active member of the Vodou community. His popularity grew since he was reputable for healing and fortune-telling. Another popular figure is Marie Laveau, who became a legend in Voodoo culture in New Orleans. Dr. John was Marie Laveau's mentor. She helped a l0t of enslaved people and attended mass regularly as she was a dedicated Catholic. Vodou religion continues to evolve in the US since many people with African origins still believe in their culture.

The Yoruba religion has led to the emergence of different belief systems, such as in Cuba (Santeríal Lucumí, Palo) and Brazil (Umbanda, Candomblé). It is also connected to other less-known religions like Vodou in Haiti and Vodoo in New Orleans. We have discussed how the Yoruba religion has influenced various African Diaspora religions. Yoruba is recognized as a religion to reckon with in many parts of the world.

Supreme Deities Bonus: Orisha Offerings Cheat Sheet

Suppose you're new to the world of Yoruba. In that case, the chances are that you find it challenging to remember all the Orisha and differentiate between them. Fortunately, you can refer to this bonus cheat sheet whenever you need a quick recap on the various Orisha, their symbols, and their appropriate offerings.

Supreme Deities

Orisha	Symbols and Roles	Appropriate Offering
Olodumare	The supreme creator	Olodumare is worshiped through the other Orishas, which is why he has no shrine or image, and no sacrifices or offerings are made directly to him.

	Not bound by a certain gender	He is not involved in humanity, at least directly, which is why he isn't worshiped.
	He created the concept of delegating	Some people choose to worship Olodumare directly, especially the priests.
	He created the orishas, who are considered intermediary spirits or deities.	The priests give offerings and pray to him; however, little is known about that subject.
	Each orisha has a certain role and dominates a specific area of life.	
	The supreme creator is omnipotent.	
	He isn't directly involved in mundane issues and lets the other Orishas handle earthly matters instead.	

Ọlọ́run	The ruler of the heavens.	Since Olorun is a manifestation of Olodumare, he, too, isn't directly worshiped.
	He is a manifestation of the supreme creator or Olodumare	He is aloof, distant, and isn't at all involved in human life.
		Olorun doesn't have any shrines and can't really accept sacrifices or offerings.
		If you wish to offer him, you can send him prayers.
Olofi	Olofi is yet another manifestation of Olodumare.	You can't directly worship Olofi nor send him offerings.
	He is considered the conduit between heaven and Earth, or Orún and Ayé, respectively.	
Nana Buluku	The female supreme deity	Mandrakes
	The root ancestress	Roses

		She is a severe spirit- the witch of the old swamp	Swamp plants
		She can't go inside, as she is too volatile	Other root plants
		The mother of Mawu, the spirit of the Moon, and Lisa, the spirit of the Sun.	
		She is also the mother of the entire universe.	
		She rules the primeval swamp that she is believed to emerge out of.	
		Associations: marches, swamps, clay, and mood	
		Nana Buluku is a divine herbalist. She is the patron of medicinal plants.	
		She has medicinal and magical powers that she can use to	

	heal the ill. She can cure the diseases that medical professionals are unable to identify, locate, or heal.
	When angered, she can bring about illnesses, especially those with swollen abdomens.
	Symbols: staffs made of palm fonds and decorated using cowrie shells.
	Trees: camwood or African sandalwood
	Stone: tourmaline
	Colors: black, pink, dark blue, and white
	Sacred numbers: 7 and 9

Olodumare and his manifestations aren't directly worshiped because they're too abstract of a concept. It is debated that humans can't grasp the significance of Olodumare as an entity, as he is the most complex spiritual being there is. According to the Yoruba religion, Olodumare, Olorun, and Olofi are incredibly immense beings that are way too immense for the human mind to comprehend. This is why the supreme deity is better broken down into multiple entities that can each exert dominion over particular aspects of life.

Female Orishas

Orisha	Symbols and Roles	Appropriate Offering
Aja	Aja is also known as the wild wind	Aja is a minor Yoruba deity, which is why there isn't much information on how to honor her or what to use as an offering to her.
	She is an orisha and the spirit of herbal healers, the forest, and the animal.	However, we believe that educating others and sharing your knowledge can be a good way to honor the deity.
	She was a herbal healer herself. She mixed the roots and herbs of multiple plants to find cures for those who were sick.	

	She liked to share her knowledge with people who were keen on learning	
	Aja was believed to be a shaman in training.	
	It is said that those who received the education of Aja came back as a Babalawo.	
	She is believed to be one of the rarest Earth gods, and that is perhaps why so little is known about her.	
	She was considered one of the first female doctors of Ocha.	
	She uses the harp, which she has mastered, to convey her messages.	

Aje	Orisha of trade, cash, and wealth	Aje is a minor deity, which is why little is known about her preferred offerings.
	Manifests in both male and female forms	There isn't a specific material element that you can offer to Aje.
	Symbols: tiger cowrie shell	However, you can live by these three principles in her honor: 1. Share everything you have 2. Don't speak about your wealth or display it 3. Don't use herbs or mess with herbalism without having sufficient knowledge about it. You should also use divine authorization.
	Associations: favors, blessings, and protection	You can recite poems about her

	Dominance: wealth and financial stability	
	Color: white	
Ayao	Orisha of the whirlwind	Ayao is a minor deity, which is why there isn't a lot of information on what should be offered to Ayao. However, you can throw a banquet in her honor.
	Associations: magical knowledge and witchcraft	
	Patron of botanicals and mystical knowledge, which she adopted from being closely acquainted with Osain, the orisha of plants.	
	Symbol: crossbow	
	Colors: green and brown	
	Sacred number: 9	
	Lives in the clouds in the sky, the eye of the tornado, and	

	the forest	
Egungun-Oya	Orisha of divination	Food and gifts can be offered to her and the dead,
	Associations: death, ghosts, destiny, truth, divination, and foresight.	Hang pictures of your loved ones who have passed away and light a candle.
	Mother of the dead	Watch the flame. If it burns out quickly without your interference, you're probably biting off more than you can chew. If the blame burns steadily and brightly, longevity and health are coming in for you. Blue flames that are average-sized suggest that you are in the company of spirits and that you'll live the average life-span.

	Mistress of spiritual destinies	To get rid of unwanted spirits, bring the candle to any light source (like a window) and ask the deity to guide the ghosts out of your house.
	Ruler of fate	
	Symbols: fire and dance	
	She can protect you from the spirits	
Mawu	Continuer of creation	It's not exactly clear what you can offer Mawu the Orisha
	The secondary creator and daughter of Nana Buluku	However, many people recite positive affirmations in honor of the deity.
	Associations: sun, moon, creativity, passion, universal law, birth, inspiration, and abundance	You can recite affirmations on happiness, love, healing, strength, joy, and empowerment.
	Symbols: the moon and clay	

Ọbà	Spirit of the river	Candles
	Associations: love, faithful wives, neglected women	Flowers
	Symbols: the sword of the machete, water buffalo, lightning, the flywhisk	Wine
	Element: water	Lake water
	Colors: white, pink, and red	Pond water
		Avoid offering her rainwater or spring water.
		You can cook beans for her.
Olókun	Orisha of the sea	Saltwater
	Spirit of life and death	Seashells
	Dominance: fertility, abundance, prosperity, health,	Other marine elements

	and healing	
	Associations: wealth, water, and health	
	Element: water	
	Colors: coral green, dark blue, and red	
	Sacred number: 7	
Ọ̀ṣun	Spirit of sweet water	Mirrors, makeup, perfume, brushes, and all other things related to feminine beauty
	Dominance: honey, love, water, mother's milk, and money	Fans made of peacock feathers
	Sacred number: 5	Yellow sandalwood fans
	Associations: love, beauty, wealth, romance, magic, and abundance	Flowers

	Symbol: a pot that contains river water	Chamomile tea
	Colors: all the shades of yellow, orange, and gold	Spinach with shrimp
	Plants: marigold, lantana, yellow squash, pumpkins, and rosemary	Honey- make sure to open the jar and taste the honey before you offer it to her. Someone had previously attempted to poison Osun through a honey offering. She will reject your offering of honey if you don't taste it first.
	Jewels: coral and amber	Orange and yellow fruit
		Orange and yellow vegetables
Ọya	Orisha of the wind, violent storms, and lighting	Purple plums
	Guardian of the gates of death	Starfruit

	She doesn't represent death. She is representative of air	Black grapes
	Master of disguise, especially as a buffalo	Purple grapes
	Associations: rebirth and death	Black-eyed peas
	Symbols: lightning bolt, thunderbolt, buffalo, wind, tornadoes, and fire	Nine eggplants- you can also slice one eggplant into nine pieces.
	Colors: maroon	Meals that incorporate eggplants- are typically served with nine-bean soup and rice.
	Sacred number: 9	Red wine
	Metal: copper	The offerings can be presented at a home altar or the cemetery gates.
	Tree: camwood and akoko	

	Plants: cypress, camphor, marigold, flamboyant, and mimosa	
Yemọja	Queen of the Sea The mother of most of the Orishas Dominance: reproductive and fertility problems, domestic violence protection, sea travel Associations: women and children, benevolence, generosity Symbols: seashells and other marine symbols Colors: white and blue Sacred number: 7 Plants: water hyacinth, seaweed, and indigo Crystals and minerals: coral, quartz crystals, and	Jewelry Perfume Scented soap. It must be new and unwrapped Flowers, particularly white roses Pomegranates, watermelon, and other wet and seedy fruits Pork cracklins Banana chips Plantain chips Poundcake Coconut cake Drizzle molasses over everything Sea creatures

	pearls	

Male Orishas

Orisha	Symbols and Roles	Appropriate Offering
Aganjú	Spirit of the forces of the Earth, especially those that are powerful and violent	Nine crackers and red palm oil
	Orisha of Volcanoes	Nine fruits
	Associations: transportation and travel. His displeasure is associated with aneurysms, traffic accidents, sudden strokes, and high blood pressure	Nine plantains served with red palm oil
	Color: red	Nine handkerchiefs
	Sacred numbers: 9 and 16	Nine silk pockets
		The handkerchiefs and silk pockets

		must be folded in squares. Each one should be in a different solid color.
Babalú Ayé	Father of the Earth	Roasted corn
	The spirit of smallpox and disease- he protects against the disease he represents	Popcorn
	He represents the ailment and its vaccine	Sesame seeds
	Dominance: minor and major skin ailments, infections, and diseases.	Cookies
	Associations: death, cemeteries, diseases.	Candy
	Sacred Number: 17	Cigars
	Colors: vary according to tradition- white, brown, black, red, yellow, and purple	Cowrie shells

	Plant: cactus	Babalu drinks
	Tree: Odan	Fine white wine
		Chicken
		If you're seeking him for healing, offer him Milagros (small religious folk charms). If he answers, offer more
		Don't offer water
Erinlẹ̀	Orisha of fertility, abundance, and wealth	Tiny metal charms in the shape of fish
	Spirit of the bush	Images of sparkly fish
	Underwater king	Images of sparkly fish
	Sacred number: 7	Swedish fish candy
	Symbols: cowries, fishing rods, and bows and arrows	

	Associations: Earth, the universe and its natural laws, hunting, and wealth		
	Colors: turquoise, indigo, coral		
	Mineral: Gold		
Èṣù	God of roads, especially crossroads	Candy	
	Protector of travelers	Rum	
	Dominance: fortune and misfortune, and divine law	Toys	
	Colors: red and black	Spicy food	
	Sacred number: 3	Cigarettes	
	Symbols: crutches, canes, cross, and key	Food with peppers and hot sauce	
	Tree: calabash		

	Plants: seedlings, vira mundo aroma, curujey, guava, guira cimarrona, camphor, cress, and cat's claw scent	
	Associations: natural laws, divine laws, and orderliness	
Ibeji	Representative of pair of twins	Toys
	Orishas of the divine twins	Sweets
	Sacred numbers: 2, 4, and 8	Anything fun
	Colors: red and blue	Fruit
	Associations: mischief, abundance, and joy	Yellow rice
	Symbols: twin dolls	Sugarcane
	They are kids	Black-eyed peas

		Okra
		Drinks and fruit juices
		Things served in pairs
		Small bananas-manzanos
		Cakes
		Chicken and rice
Ọbàtálá	The father of the sky	His diet is bland and restricted.
	The creator of human bodies	Hates salt and spicy food.
	The oldest of all Orishas	Prefers white or light-colored offerings.
	The king of religion in heaven, or Orun	Rice
	Color: white	Coconut
	Sacred number: 8	Eggs

	Dominance: purity	Cocoa butter
	Associations: purpose, peace, honesty, purity, resurrection, the New Year, and forgiveness	White yams
	Symbols: white crown, staff, dove	Meringues
	Plants: acacia, barberry, bell, cotton, atipola, bayonet, scourer, may flower, soursop, and white, mauve.	White sacrifices like hens, female goats, and doves.
Oduduwa	The first king of Oyo	He eats with Obbatala, the white Orisha, and accepts sacrifices like:
	The oldest dead man	• White goats
	The lord of desires	• Hens • Guinea pigs
	A creator, a justice doer	• Quails • Pigeons
	Associations: death, purity, harmony,	

	creation, and energy	
	Colors: white and opal	
Ògún	Primordial Orisha	He will eat just about anything due to his big appetite
	The first king of Ife	Plantains
	The god of war and metals	Jutia (small rodents)
	Dominance: transformation, function, and life	Smoked fish
	Associations: tools, creativity, and intelligence	Pomegranates
	Sacred numbers: 3 and 7	Watermelons
	Colors: red, black, and green	Rum
	Plants: cyperus esculentus, garlic, rosemary, chile pepper, black	Grapes

	pepper, and other medicinal herbs	
	Trees: akoko, camwood, palm, eucalyptus, and calabash	Gin
	Symbols: palm frond, iron, and the dog	Bananas
		Pigeons
		He-goat
		roosters
Oko	The Orisha of agriculture, farming, and fertility	All crops, especially root vegetables
	Dominance: life, earth, and death	Yams
	Associations: health, vitality, and stability	Sweet potatoes
	Colors: red, white, pink, and light blue	Corn
	Sacred number: 7	Taro root

		Palm oil seasoned foods
		Toasted corn
		Smoked fish
Osanyin	The Orisha of nature	Coins
	Healing herbs	Alcohol, especially aguardiente
	Colors: green, red, white, and yellow	Rum
	Sacred numbers: 6, 21, and 7	Candles
	Dominance: forests, herbalism, healing, and wild areas	Tobacco
	Associations: plants, magic, talking, and healing	
	Symbols: twisted tree branches and pipes	
	Multi-colored beads	

Oṣùmàrè	Divine serpent Orisha of the rainbow, transformation, serpent, and cycles	Corn
		Cowries
		Shrimp sauteed in dende oil
	Guardian and protector of children	Beans
		Pure water
		Roosters and armadillo
	Colors: yellow, purple, burgundy, pink, and green	Peanuts
		Yams
	Dominance: permeance and wealth	Sweet potatoes
	Associations: regenerations, transformation, and rebirth	
	Symbols: serpents and rainbows	
	Cowrie shells, iron, yellow, and green glass beads	
Ọ̀ṣọ́ọ̀sì	The spirits of meals, as he is the provider of food.	He loves to be offered hunted animals, like cooked pigs, guinea fowl, quails, deer, pigeons, and goats.

	Orisha of contemplation and the patron of arts and all things beautiful	Grapes
	Colors: Blue in Ketu and green elsewhere	Pears
	Sacred numbers: 3, 4, and 7	Smoked fish
	Dominance: forests, hunts, wealth, and animals	Plantains
	Associations: craftiness, wisdom, lightness, and astuteness when hunting.	Pomegranates
	Plants: strenna white, scorpionfish, partridge vine, coral, enchantment, coast incense, prodigious, yellow cabin	Bananas
	Symbols: crossbow	Anisette

	and arrow	Jutia
		Sweet potato fries
		cigar
Shango	The father of the sky	Rum
	The god of thunder and lightning	Whiskey- some recommend Jack Daniels, in particular.
	Colors: Red, gold, and white	Beer
	Sacred numbers:4 and 6	Tobacco
	Dominance: human vitality and male sexuality	Chili
	Stones: carnelian, fire opals, diamonds, and gold.	Peppers
	Associations: protection, drumming, justice, life, magick, fire, thunder, lightning,	Hot and spicy food

	and virility.	
	Plants: chili peppers, red oak trees, marijuana, hibiscus, chinaberry, and sassafras.	Gunpowder
	Symbols: thunderstorms, red and white bead necklaces, lightning bolts, and double-headed axes.	Meat

There are numerous Yoruba Orishas, each of which rules a certain aspect of life. Each Orisha demands unique offerings and has different characteristics and temperaments. This makes it impossible for most people, especially those new to this belief system, to always remember who is who. Fortunately, you can always refer to this cheat sheet whenever you need to be reminded of the deities and all their aspects.

Conclusion

The Yoruba religion is one of the most fascinating religions in the world. It is filled with legends, myths, and magic. In this book, we have covered everything that you would want to know about the enchanting world of the Ìṣẹ̀ṣe. We have provided information about its history and culture, so you have enough background to start your learning journey. You also learned about Olorun, the Supreme God, and the creation myth.

The world of the Orishas is probably the most interesting part of the Yoruba religion. As the intercessors between humans and the Supreme God, Orishas play a huge role in helping people communicate with Oldorun. To call on the Orishas and take advantage of their powers, you first need to know who they are and how they can help you. All the information to help you navigate their world, including how many Orishas there are – and which are the most helpful and important ones – has been discussed.

All gods prefer offerings and sacrifices, and Orishas are no different. Learning about how you can appease these gods will be beneficial when you call on them to ask for their assistance. There are male and female Orishas, each with a fascinating history and legends behind them. Whether you are sick, want a child, or looking for love, you'll find an Orisha willing to help. As giving as

Orishas are, some of them can be angry and destructive, and we have the information you need to navigate your way through the Orishas you should never anger or provoke. Just like people, some Orishas don't get along with each other. Learning about their history will help you avoid venerating rival Orishas together like Oya and Oshun.

In the next part of the book, we talked about the practice of Ifa divination and how it works. You read about the diviner Babalawo and whether anyone can become one. Additionally, we covered the importance of ancestors in the Yoruba religion. We need to honor our ancestors and seek their wisdom to help us navigate life. We talked about venerating them, which usually occurs on an altar. After finishing chapter 7, you'll be ready to create an altar or shrine dedicated to your ancestors.

Every religion has its calendar and holy days. Each day of the week is called something different and has a different meaning in the Yoruba religion. To practice this religion, you need to learn about its various holidays so you can celebrate them with your loved ones. We provided all of the information you need regarding important festivals as well. There are also many Yoruba spells and rituals that you should learn about, and in this book, you'll find all of the ingredients and instructions you need to start practicing.

Yoruba is a religion rich in legends, myths, gods, and magic. It has become a huge influence on other religions all over the world. Now you've learned about many of these other beliefs, what they have in common with Yoruba, and what sets them apart. There is so much about the Yoruba religion out there; we hope we've brought you all of the essential information you'll need to learn about your spiritual heritage. Good luck on your journey!

Here's another book by Mari Silva that you might like

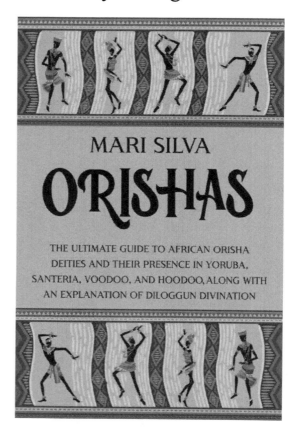

MARI SILVA

ORISHAS

THE ULTIMATE GUIDE TO AFRICAN ORISHA
DEITIES AND THEIR PRESENCE IN YORUBA,
SANTERIA, VOODOO, AND HOODOO, ALONG WITH
AN EXPLANATION OF DILOGGUN DIVINATION

Su regalo gratuito

¡Gracias por descargar este libro! Si desea aprender más acerca de varios temas de espiritualidad, entonces únase a la comunidad de Mari Silva y obtenga el MP3 de meditación guiada para despertar su tercer ojo. Este MP3 de meditación guiada está diseñado para abrir y fortalecer el tercer ojo para que pueda experimentar un estado superior de conciencia.

https://livetolearn.lpages.co/mari-silva-third-eye-meditation-mp3-spanish/

References

15 facts on African religions. (2014, May 16). https://blog.oup.com/2014/05/15-facts-on-african-religions/

Google Arts & Culture. (n.d.). Yoruba people of west Africa. Google Arts & Culture website: https://artsandculture.google.com/usergallery/EQKyzgLnW1j4IQ

Sawe, B. E. (2019, April 17). What is the Yoruba religion? Yoruba beliefs and origin. WorldAtlas website: https://www.worldatlas.com/articles/what-is-the-yoruba-religion.html

Yoruba Religion. (n.d.). Encyclopedia.com website:

https://www.encyclopedia.com/environment/encyclopedias-almanacs-transcripts-and-maps/yoruba-religion

Rodríguez, C. (2020, August 11). Who are Olofin Olorun and Olodumare? Ashé pa mi Cuba. https://ashepamicuba.com/en/quienes-son-olofin-olorun-y-olodumare

Wigington, P. (n.d.). Yoruba religion: History and beliefs. Learn Religions.

https://www.learnreligions.com/yoruba-religion-4777660

Cuba, A. pa mi. (2020, July 9). What is an Ebbó? Types and Meanings of this Sacred Astral Cleansing. Ashé pa mi Cuba. https://ashepamicuba.com/en/que-es-un-ebbo-tipos-y-significado

Religion. (n.d.). Jrank.Org. https://science.jrank.org/pages/11051/Religion-African-Diaspora-Spiritual-Assets-Ase-Konesans.html

Rodríguez, C. (2020a, August 1). What is Irunmole? The rise of the Orisha. Ashé pa mi Cuba. https://ashepamicuba.com/en/que-es-irunmole-el-surgimiento-del-orisha

Rodríguez, C. (2020b, August 25). Is there a difference between Orisha and Irunmole? Ashé pa mi Cuba. https://ashepamicuba.com/en/diferencia-entre-orisha-e-irunmole

Who are the Orishas? (2016, September 20). DJONIBA Dance Center.

https://www.djoniba.com/who-are-the-orishas

Wigington, P. (n.d.). Yoruba religion: History and beliefs. Learn Religions.

https://www.learnreligions.com/yoruba-religion-4777660

Abata – occult world. (n.d.). Occult-World.Com. https://occult-world.com/abata

Ancient Code Team. (2014, December 16). Goddesses Of Yoruba Mythology. Ancient Code. https://www.ancient-code.com/goddesses-yoruba-mythology

Asterope. (n.d.). Deity of the Week. Blogspot.Com.

https://deity-of-the-week.blogspot.com/search?q=ayao

Ayao – occult world. (n.d.). Occult-World.Com. https://occult-world.com/ayao

Deities of the Yoruba and Fon Religions. (n.d.). Encyclopedia.Com.

https://www.encyclopedia.com/history/news-wires-white-papers-and-books/deities-yoruba-and-fon-religions

Fernández, N. C. (2020, September 12). The Orisha Abata, the entwined Serpent that complements Inle. Ashé pa mi Cuba. https://ashepamicuba.com/en/abata-orisha

Francisca, U. (2020, December 22). See why Olokun is the owner of the deep sea. XoticBrands Home Decor. https://www.xoticbrands.net/blogs/news/olokun

Goddess Oba. (2012, February 26). Journeying to the Goddess. https://journeyingtothegoddess.wordpress.com/2012/02/26/goddess-oba

Iwalaiye, T. (2021, October 22). African Gods: Who is the goddess, Oya? Pulse Nigeria. https://www.pulse.ng/lifestyle/food-travel/african-gods-who-is-the-goddess-oya/q5gf7h2

Konkwo, R. (2018, June 18). Yoruba Gods and Goddesses. Legit.Ng – Nigeria News. https://www.legit.ng/1175618-yoruba-gods-goddesses.html

Nana buruku – occult world. (n.d.). Occult-World.Com. https://occult-world.com/nana-buruku

Rodríguez, C. (2020, October 13). Who is Aha? The Orisha of the Whirlwind and the Wild Wind. Ashé pa mi Cuba. https://ashepamicuba.com/en/orisha-aja

Thafeng, V. A. P. by. (2021, September 6). The mythical origins of the African Goddesses in West African societies. Yoair Blog. https://www.yoair.com/blog/the-mythical-origins-of-the-african-goddesses-in-west-african-societies

Timesofindia. (2021, January 22). Inspiring goddesses from mythology. Times of India. https://timesofindia.indiatimes.com/life-style/books/web-stories/inspiring-goddesses-from-mythology/photostory/80407777.cms

Visit profile. (2012, August 25). West African god and goddess (2). Blogspot.Com.

https://kwekudee-tripdownmemorylane.blogspot.com/2012/08/sculptured-impression-of-olorun-1_25.html

Walker, S. (2021, April 27). The ancient beliefs of African goddesses. Amplify Africa. https://www.amplifyafrica.org/post/the-ancient-beliefs-of-african-goddesses

Yewa – Yoruba Goddess of virginity and death. (2021, October 26). Symbol Sage.

https://symbolsage.com/yewa-goddess-of-death

About: Erinlẹ. (n.d.). DBpedia. https://dbpedia.org/page/Erinl%E1%BA%B9

Adoga, J., & Gbolahan, A. (2020). Oduduwa. Lulu.com.

Aganju. (n.d.). Gods & Goddess Wiki. https://gods-goddess.fandom.com/wiki/Aganju

Aganju: The deified 4th Alaafin of Oyo. (2019, September 27). WELCOME TO MY WOVEN WORDS. https://mywovenwords.com/2019/09/aganju-the-deified-4th-alaafin-of-oyo.html

Canizares, R., & Lerner, A. E. (2000a). Babalu aye: Santeria and the lord of pestilence. Original Publications.

Canizares, R., & Lerner, A. E. (2000b). Babalu aye: Santeria and the lord of pestilence. Original Publications.

Dennett, R. E. (2019). Eshu. In Nigerian Studies (pp. 94–96). Routledge.

Erinle – occult world. (n.d.). Occult-World.Com. https://occult-world.com/erinle

Joiner-Siedlak, M. (2018, December 17). Babalu Aye – the god of diseases. Monique Joiner Siedlak. https://mojosiedlak.com/babalu-aye-god-diseases

Joiner-Siedlak, M. (2019, September 27). The sacred twins – Ibeji. Monique Joiner Siedlak.

https://mojosiedlak.com/the-sacred-twins-ibeji

Konkwo, R. (2018, June 18). Yoruba Gods and Goddesses. Legit.Ng – Nigeria News.

https://www.legit.ng/1175618-yoruba-gods-goddesses.html

Mark, J. J. (2021). Orisha. World History Encyclopedia. https://www.worldhistory.org/Orisha

Nut_Meg. (n.d.). Erinle. Obsidianportal.Com.

https://god-touched.obsidianportal.com/characters/erinle

Rodríguez, C. (2021, January 5). 10 elements about Oduduwá: Deity who rules the secrets of death. Ashé pa mi Cuba. https://ashepamicuba.com/en/oduduwa-caracteristicas

Ṣàngó. (n.d.). Afropeans.Com. https://afropeans.com/kitchen/%E1%B9%A3ango-yoruba-god-of-thunder

The 5 most influential orishas. (2019, August 11). The Guardian Nigeria News – Nigeria and

World News. https://guardian.ng/life/the-5-most-influential-orishas

The Editors of Encyclopedia Britannica. (2015). Eshu. In Encyclopedia Britannica.

Curnow, K. (n.d.). Chapter 3.6: Art and divination. In The Bright Continent: African Art History. Msl Academic Endeavors.

Divination techniques. (n.d.). Uiowa.edu website:

https://africa.uima.uiowa.edu/chapters/divination/divination-techniques/?start=1

Santo, D. E. (2019). Divination. Cambridge Encyclopedia of Anthropology.

https://www.anthroencyclopedia.com/entry/divination

Ost, B. (2021). LibGuides: African traditional religions textbook: Ifa: Chapter 5. Our ancestors are with us now. https://research.auctr.edu/c.php?g=1122253&p=8185273

Egun / The ancestors – The Yoruba Religious Concepts. (n.d.). Google.com website: https://sites.google.com/site/theyorubareligiousconcepts/egungun-the-ancestors

Contributed by Kalila Borghini, L. (2010, June 9). Offerings and sacrifices: Honoring our ancestors helps us give thanks. GoodTherapy.org Therapy Blog website: https://www.goodtherapy.org/blog/offerings

The new exhibit pushes viewers to connect with an African tradition of honoring ancestors. (n.d.). Wisc.edu website: https://news.wisc.edu/new-exhibit-pushes-viewers-to-connect-with-an-african-tradition-of-honoring-ancestors

Cuba, A. pa mi. (2021, February 11). The Orishas, their Syncretism, and Yoruba Calendar of celebrations. Ashé pa mi Cuba. https://ashepamicuba.com/en/calendario-yoruba

Editors. (2021, December 10). Yoruba New Year. New York Latin Culture MagazineTM. https://www.newyorklatinculture.com/yoruba-new-year

Ifa Orisha Egbe Ile Tiwalade Yoruba Community of Metro Atlanta, Georgia. (n.d.). Egbe Tiwalade. http://egbetiwalade.weebly.com/yoruba-calendar.html

Kim, A. (n.d.). How does the Yoruba calendar work? – Theburningofrome.com. Theburningofrome.Com. https://www.theburningofrome.com/trending/how-does-the-yoruba-calendar-work

NIGERIA HIGH COMMISSION. (n.d.). Nhcjamaica.Org. https://nhcjamaica.org/festivals.html

Olawale, J. (2018, January 5). Yoruba festivals and holidays in Nigeria. Legit.Ng – Nigeria News. https://www.legit.ng/1143388-yoruba-festivals-holidays-nigeria.html

Oro: A Yoruba festival that is anti-women. (2018, May 7). The Guardian Nigeria News – Nigeria and World News. https://guardian.ng/life/oro-a-yoruba-festival-that-is-anti-women

RajKumar. (2021a, April 16). Months of the year in Yoruba. Happy Days 365.

https://happydays365.org/months-of-the-year/months-in-yoruba

RajKumar. (2021b, June 18). Days of the Week in Yoruba. Happy Days 365.

https://happydays365.org/days-of-the-week/weekdays-in-yoruba

Surhone, L. M., Timpledon, M. T., & Marseken, S. F. (Eds.). (2010). Yoruba Calendar. Betascript Publishing.

The Centenary Project. (n.d.). New yam festival: A celebration of life and culture. Google Arts & Culture. https://artsandculture.google.com/story/new-yam-festival-a-celebration-of-life-and-culture-pan-atlantic-university/vgUhxQmEwWsNLQ?hl=en

Babalola, A. B., Ogunfolakan, A., & Lababidi, L. (2020, October 29). Rituals, Religious practices, and glass/glass bead making in Ile-Ife and Bida, Nigeria. Endangered Material Knowledge Programme. https://www.emkp.org/rituals-religious-practices-and-glass-glass-bead-making-in-ile-ife-and-bida-nigeria

How to invoke the energy of yorube goddess Oshun. (n.d.). Vice.Com.

https://www.vice.com/en/article/3kjepv/how-to-invoke-oshun-yoruba-goddess-orisha

mythictreasures. (2020, May 10). Introduction to 7 day candles. Mythictreasures.

https://www.mythictreasures.com/post/into-to-7-day-candles

Urošević, A. (2015, September 23). Spiritual cleansing in Ifá: "sour" and "sweet" baths. Amor et Mortem.

https://amoretmortem.wordpress.com/2015/09/23/spiritual-cleansing-in-Ifa-sour-and-sweet-baths

Brandon, G. (2018). orisha. In Encyclopedia Britannica.

"Santeria": La Regla de Ocha-Ifa and lukumi. (n.d.). Pluralism.org website:
https://pluralism.org/%E2%80%9Csanter%C3%ADa%E2%80%9D-the-lucumi-way

Dialogue Institute. (n.d.). Afro-Caribbean and African religion information —.Dialogue Institute website:
https://dialogueinstitute.org/afrocaribbean-and-african-religion-information

Currents Staff. (n.d.). African-based religions: Santeria, Candomble, vodoun. Riverwestcurrents.org website:
https://riverwestcurrents.org/2006/04/african-based-religions-santeria-candomble-vodoun.html

Aganyu – occult world. (n.d.). Occult-world.com website:
https://occult-world.com/aganyu

Ajé-shaluga – occult world. (n.d.). Occult-world.com website:
https://occult-world.com/aje-shaluga

Asterope. (n.d.). Deity of the Week. Blogspot.com website:
http://deity-of-the-week.blogspot.com/search/label/yoruban

Ayao – occult world. (n.d.). Occult-world.com website:
https://occult-world.com/ayao

Babalu ayé – occult world. (n.d.). Occult-world.com website:
https://occult-world.com/babalu-aye

Coburg, A. (2012). Osain: Cantos a osain (1st ed.).
http://readersandrootworkers.org/wiki/Osain

Eshu elegbara – occult world. (n.d.). Occult-world.com website:
https://occult-world.com/eshu-elegbara

evelynna. (n.d.). Oxumaré written by Evelynn Amabeoku. Blogspot.com website:

http://ucrpandas.blogspot.com/2009/05/oxumare-written-by-evelynn-amabeoku.html

Fatunmbi, L. (2000). Ochosi: IFA and the spirit of the tracker. Plainview, NY: Original

Publications.

Fatunmbi, L., & Canizares, R. (2000). Obatala: Santeria and the white-robed king of the Orisha. Plainview, NY: Original Publications.

Fernández, N. C. (2020, December 11). Do you know the Sacred Herbs of Oshosi? 8 Plants you should know. Ashé pa mi Cuba website: https://ashepamicuba.com/en/hierbas-de-oshosi

Fernández, N. C. (2021, January 10). Ayana, Aja, and Ayao: Three very powerful minor deities of the Osha. Ashé pa mi Cuba website: https://ashepamicuba.com/en/ayana-aja-y-ayao

Goddess Egungun-Oya. (2012, June 6). Journeying to the Goddess website:

https://journeyingtothegoddess.wordpress.com/2012/06/06/goddess-egungun-oya

Ibeji – occult world. (n.d.). Occult-world.com website: https://occult-world.com/ibeji

Joiner-Siedlak, M. (2019, June 6). Ochosi – the Hunter. Monique Joiner Siedlak website:

https://mojosiedlak.com/ochosi-the-hunter

Mark, J. J. (2021). Orisha. World History Encyclopedia. https://www.worldhistory.org/Orisha

Mawu mother earth. (2013, August 27). Moon Mothers of Half Moon Bay website:

https://moonmothers.org/2013/08/27/mawu-mother-earth

Mawu-Lisa – occult world. (n.d.). Occult-world.com website: https://occult-world.com/mawu-lisa

"Mawu's themes are creativity, Universal Law, passion, abundance, birth, and inspiration. Her symbols are clay and .... (n.d.). Pinterest website:
https://www.pinterest.com/pin/54254370495561047

Melissa. (2018, March 17). Oshumare – the sacred serpent. Afro-diasporic Religiosity website:
https://candombleusa.wordpress.com/2018/03/17/oshumare-the-sacred-serpent

Nana buruku – occult world. (n.d.). Occult-world.com website:
https://occult-world.com/nana-buruku

Oba – occult world. (n.d.). Occult-world.com website: https://occult-world.com/oba

Ogun. (n.d.). Santeria Church of the Orishas website:
http://santeriachurch.org/the-orishas/ogun

Ogun – occult world. (n.d.). Occult-world.com website:
https://occult-world.com/ogun

OLODUMARE – the Yoruba Religious concepts. (n.d.).
Google.com website:
https://sites.google.com/site/theyorubareligiousconcepts/olodumare

Olokun – occult world. (n.d.). Occult-world.com website:
https://occult-world.com/olokun

Orisha – occult world. (n.d.). Occult-world.com website:
https://occult-world.com/orisha

Orisha Oko. (n.d.). Santeria Church of the Orishas website:
http://santeriachurch.org/the-orishas/orisha-oko

Orisha oko – occult world. (n.d.). Occult-world.com website:
https://occult-world.com/orisha-oko

Osain – occult world. (n.d.). Occult-world.com website:
https://occult-world.com/osain

Oshumare – occult world. (n.d.). Occult-world.com website: https://occult-world.com/oshumare

Oshun – occult world. (n.d.). Occult-world.com website: https://occult-world.com/oshun

Oya – occult world. (n.d.). Occult-world.com website: https://occult-world.com/oya

Purple Moon – Orisha Osain. (n.d.). Pmtarot.com website: https://www.pmtarot.com/m/showproduct.php?p=07278&c=&lang=eng

Rodríguez, C. (2020a, August 24). SUBSCRIBE FOR FREE Eleguá is the Orisha eternal guardian of the roads and Read more. Ashé pa mi Cuba website: https://ashepamicuba.com/en/plantas-de-elegua

Rodríguez, C. (2020b, August 27). 10 representative plants of Obatalá. Ashé pa mi Cuba website: https://ashepamicuba.com/en/plantas-de-obatala

Rodríguez, C. (2021, January 5). 10 elements about Oduduwá: Deity who rules the secrets of death. Ashé pa mi Cuba website: https://ashepamicuba.com/en/oduduwa-caracteristicas

SAGE reference – encyclopedia of African religion. (n.d.). Sagepub.com website: https://sk.sagepub.com/reference/africanreligion/n323.xml

templeofathena. (2016, September 9). GMC: Orisha Osumare. Temple of Athena the Savior website: https://templeofathena.wordpress.com/2016/09/09/gmc-orisha-osumare

The Afro-Cuban Orisha pantheon. (n.d.). Historymiami.org website: http://www.historymiami.org/online-exhibits/orisha/english/pantheon.htm

Vaughan, S. A. (2017). Ibeji. http://santeriachurch.org/the-orishas/ibeji /

Visit profile. (2013, December 11). Olokun deity and its various olokun festivals. Blogspot.com website: https://kwekudee-tripdownmemorylane.blogspot.com/2013/12/olokun-deity-and-its-various-olokun.html

Yemaya – occult world. (n.d.). Occult-world.com website: https://occult-world.com/yemaya

Made in the USA
Las Vegas, NV
30 November 2023